Gardening for beginners

3 BOOKS IN 1: GARDENING IN CONTAINERS, COMPANION PLANTING AND HYDROPONIC.
EVERYTHING YOU NEED TO KNOW TO GROW HEALTHY VEGETABLES, FRUITS AND HERBS EASILY AT HOME

BY EDWARD GREEN

Table of Contents

VEGETABLE GARDENING IN CONTAINERS:

HOW TO SUCCESSFULLY GROW HEALTHY ORGANIC VEGETABLES, FRUITS & HERBS IN RAISED BEDS & SMALL URBAN SPACES FOR A THRIVING HOMEMADE GARDEN IN PATIOS & BALCONIES.

BY EDWARD GREEN

VEGETABLE

GARDENING

in Containers

HOW TO SUCCESSFULLY GROW HEALTHY ORGANIC
VEGETABLES, FRUITS & HERBS IN RAISED BEDS,
POTS & SMALL URBAN SPACES FOR A THRIVING
HOMEMADE GARDEN IN PATIOS & BALCONIES

EDWARD GREEN

Introduction: Vegetable Gardening in Containers

Container gardens allow you to make any area brighter and more colorful, even when the space is limited in size. You can enjoy growing plants in places where you thought it might be impossible otherwise. Containers placed in corners, suspended from ceilings, window boxes placed on railings, and even small pots placed on a shelf or bookcase are just a few examples for these types of gardens and arrangements.

If you cannot grow a vegetable garden outside of your home because of poor soil, if you are living in a limited space without access to an outdoor patio, or if you only have a small deck, you can still enjoy the simple pleasures that vegetable container gardening offers.

The increasing popularity of container gardens in different parts of the world has taught many people the benefits of cultivating these masterpieces. You might see plants growing in containers on balconies or rooftops, in office spaces, restaurants, and more. People can create special gardens—regardless of the location or the area available to them. Additionally, individuals find they can grow special plants that may require extra attention concerning soil and water—plants they could not manage if they were part of a large garden.

Vegetables and flowers can take on an entirely new look when displayed in a container that highlights their unique shape, size, color, and texture. It offers instant color to a room any time of day, and beautiful displays of plants can often change the entire look of a space. These are some of the reasons why container gardening has become a favorite option incorporated by interior designers when dealing with areas.

Even if you have enough room in your garden outside for planting, container gardens allow you to tailor your decorations around seasonal changes. For example, if you live in a climate that experiences all four seasons, the winter may deem it necessary to move your containers inside where your plants can be protected. The portability of gardens in containers gives you the option of enjoying your foliage year round—even in an area where the weather changes dramatically.

Vegetable Container Gardening offers the option of allowing you to own a garden. It gives you the flexibility to reorder or move your plants around whenever and wherever you like. You also have the freedom to choose the plants you want to grow, whether they are flowers, vegetables, herbs, or combinations of all three. You can even grow tropical plants during the winter months if you keep the plants inside your home. Then, when the summertime comes, you can either transplant your plants outside or simply move the containers outdoors.

Creating a Vegetable container garden makes it possible for those who live in the city to enjoy eating fresh salads with the lettuce, tomatoes, and herbs they have grown. High-rise patios and porches become even more beautiful with the addition of container gardens displaying their arrays of brilliant colors and shapes.

Vegetable gardening in Containers is extremely versatile, is not difficult to achieve, and has many advantages.

Benefits from Container Gardening

Many people consider gardening in a container for several reasons. It is a desirable method of planting compared to the traditional gardening system where tilling is required. Gardeners often complain of back pain, among other health issues, as a result of too much hard work done while gardening. Container gardening offers a concept that does reduce not only the chances of having these health issues but also gives room for you to explore your creativity while planting. Here are some of the several benefits you will enjoy while growing plants in a container:

1. Know Your Food

When root tubers like carrots, potatoes, and radishes are planted, they can be easily harvested by overturning the container on a plastic sheet. It is a more comfortable and accident-free way of collecting these crops. Unlike digging them up where there is the possibility of causing damage to the plants in the process. With container gardening, harvesting has never been safer and more comfortable. Collection in container gardening is quite easy and makes the whole system more interesting.

2. Recycled Material for the Containers

Less Need for Resources

The amount of water and nutrients needed to grow plants in container successfully is less compared to traditional outdoor gardening. Growing plants in the ground requires more water and nutrient because of a larger surface area which makes the water not only spread but also susceptible to evaporation. It is not the case in the container as evaporation is minimal and therefore makes the plants require less watering. It also goes for the nutrients needed by the plants. The box requires less fertilizer application, unlike outside gardening, as long as the right size of a pot is used in growing the plants.

3. The Garden Can Be Moved If You Move To another Apartment

The Benefit of Moving the Container Around

Another advantage of this system of gardening is that it allows you to move the pot to a more suitable location. If you do not want to keep bending to the ground to attend to your plant, you can always adjust the height of your garden to suit you. If you need to move your containers to a better area from more exposure to sunlight, you can easily do so with boxes. It is a benefit that cannot be enjoyed in traditional ground farming.

You Can Grow Plants Indoor

The ability to move a container makes it easy to transfer the pots indoor. It could be either to protect them from adverse weather conditions or to give the home interior an appealing sight. Whatever the reason is, plants growing in containers can do well indoors as much as they do outdoors. Everyone knows sunlight is essential to the growth of plants, but several plants require little sunshine, and they will thrive more quickly indoors. A provision could also be made for artificial light for plants that need more light exposure than they get from the reflection of the sun. For plants to thrive indoors, the right conditions must be put in place, such as keeping the containers near a window to enjoy the reflection of the sun or supplying artificial lights. It is a significant advantage for those who are mobility-challenged or too old to work under the sun as they can enjoy what they love doing within the comfort of their home.

The versatility, accessibility, mobility, and flexibility of growing plants in the container are some of the great reasons why it is the right choice for you. You do not have to worry about your garden whenever you change the environment and move to another location. Your container can also move with you to your new home. You have the opportunity to vary your garden's color scheme and give your outdoor the attractive display you want. Container gardening doesn't require much garden tools and equipment. You can always use what you have at home and start creating your garden according to your budget, no matter how low it is.

Easier Pests and Diseases Control

The control of pests and disease is a major concern in gardening generally, especially in-ground traditional gardening. Failure to control pests and conditions will result in poor harvest or complete loss of the affected plants. The risk of this is, however, very minimal in container gardening as the effect of pests can easily be noticed and hence, controlled before it becomes a major problem. Pests and disease control in container gardening usually require little or no chemical application. It makes the harvest almost always chemical-free. In dealing with the pests, cotton buds soaked in rubbing alcohol can be used to eliminate pests like aphids, while brush can be used to remove larger insects.

The Growth of Weed Is Limited In Container Gardening

One of the disadvantages of traditional gardening is, having to put up with the weeds. It is very limited in the container if at all, it is experienced. It can also be quickly addressed without having to use toxic chemicals, which could affect the growing plants. Container gardening is, therefore, a suitable method not just for experienced gardeners but also for those with little or no experience.

The Luxury of Time and Convenience

One of the major attractions of this concept of gardening is the convenience that comes with it. It is such a secure system of farming that the elderly or those who cannot go out can adopt indoor. Unlike traditional gardening, gardening in containers gives you the luxury of time as the weather or general environmental condition does not limit them. You do not have to wait for a particular planting season before growing a specific plant. Container gardening makes it possible to grow plants anytime and anywhere as long as the right growing condition is met within the pot. Its method of gardening makes gardening an acceptable practice for everyone and anyone, regardless of how occupied they are.

The Benefit of Choosing Your Growing Medium and Creating Your Growing Condition

In container gardening, you have the opportunity to try out different types of growing mediums to get the best yield possible. Some of the growing medium you could use includes; soil, expanded clay pellets, coco coir, and peat moss. Its system of gardening allows you to create the best growing condition for your plants. You have the option of purchasing soilless potting mixes or create the increasing status of your plants. You can adjust the light, the soil pH, and nutrients to suit what the plants need for maximum yield.

The Benefit of No-till Gardening

The container provides an easier way to grow plants without having to till the ground. Anyone who has ever had to cultivate the field knows how much of hard work it is. In addition to developing being a strenuous exercise, recent studies have shown that tilling the soil affects some natural organisms which are required for the growth of the plants. It makes the concept of container gardening appreciable as it provides the opportunity of creating a suitable growing condition such that the maximum result possible is obtained without digging the ground. Container gardening helps you to save time and energy because it is a no-till kind of gardening.

A Great Solution to the Issue of Limited Space

The availability or non-availability of space is never an issue when gardening in a container. It is because this method does not require a filed or vast farmland before it can be practiced. You do not need a ground. You can have your plants growing perfectly on a window sill, or a balcony, or anywhere suitable. The maximum utilization of space is one of the top benefits of container gardening.

Why You Should Grow Organic

Today though, more gardeners are tending towards the organic path, yet there are times when non-organic gardening is necessary.

You will know from your grocery shopping that there is a difference between organic and non-organic produce, which is often reflected in the price.There is a fairly significant difference in the two approaches for the container gardener. However, you will find that organic products tend to have a better flavor.

You shouldn't feel you are pushed into organic gardening because it is "the thing to do" and should take an approach that suits you. Most gardeners tend to be mostly organic but with the occasional non-organic method thrown in.

You're growing organic when you grow plants without using chemicals for pest or weed control or fertilization. If you want your plants to be 100% organic, you can buy organic seeds and organic soil too, even though many gardeners don't go that far and will buy regular seeds and soils but opt for natural methods of caring for their plants.

Benefits of Organic Food and Gardening

The advantage of organic gardening is that it is environmentally friendly, so you are not introducing artificial and potentially dangerous chemicals into the soil. Organic fertilizer, for example, will not cause any harm to the environment and improves the quality of your land, whereas chemical fertilizers cause runoff that gets into the water system, plus they only provide a temporary boost of nutrients.

According to numerous studies, it appears that organic vegetables contain higher levels of nutrients than their non-organic counterparts. According to a 2001 study, organic produce was 27% higher in vitamin C, 29% higher in magnesium, 21% higher in iron, and 14% higher in phosphorous.

Perhaps one of the biggest advantages of organic gardening is that it is cheaper than non-organic gardening, and yet you will get a product that is more expensive when bought directly from a store. The store-bought fertilizers can be costly, yet you can make your organic fertilizers for virtually nothing! Comfrey tea, horse manure and compost can all be made from few ingredients, they are natural and they're great for your plants too. In addition, you can also integrate the companion planting method and encourage beneficial insects to your garden to help keep pests away and avoid any chemical.

The downside of organic gardening is that it is considered a harder work because many of the methods used are more time-consuming. For example, you don't use sprays to keep weeds down but pull them up by hand. You will have to learn how to do some more planning, such as for crop rotation and companion planting. Still, for me, the results are much more rewarding and the vegetables far tastier.

Also, keep in mind that you are going to plant more densely than you would in the soil. If anything with organic gardening, you get a higher yield in the smaller area because you are not dowsing your plants with potentially harmful chemicals, and you have a highly nutritious soil.

GMO (Toxic Chemicals) and Why You Should Avoid Them

Many pesticides are linked to cancer, congenital disabilities and nerve damage. In a smaller area such as a container garden, the effects are likely to be much more concentrated. Certainly, in containers, I would be as close to organic as I could not only for this reason but also because containers can be indoors or nearer to your home and so the chemicals will linger in the atmosphere. As time goes by, scientists are finding more and more health risks associated with the use of chemicals on food.

A few years ago, chemical DDT was considered safe to use on food. It was used as a pesticide and after years of use, it was discovered that this chemical was highly toxic, remained in the food and water and was causing serious illness in people.

My recommendation to you is to be as organic as you can, avoid chemical sprays and toxic chemicals, but if you need to use sprays for anything, then look for organic ones, there are plenty on the market, which are food safe. It will help avoid the build-up of potentially harmful chemicals in the vegetables you are growing.

There is no right or wrong answer to the question, "Should I grow organically?" but more and more home gardeners are moving this way to reduce their impact on the environment, to protect their health and to grow better-tasting produce.

Container Gardening

You might ask yourself why you should approach container gardening when you can plant a garden in the ground.

Why Should You Choose To Grow Your Plants In Containers?

It helps eliminate overcrowding. If you are entertaining, you can arrange the plants in different parts of the home or patio. The colors and foliage can be mixed to create different patterns and effects. Rare and unusual varieties that have special soil and light requirements can more easily care.

Aside from the visual effects of container gardening, there are other reasons, which include yard conditions. If you have ever had problems with termites or moles, container gardening is certainly the key. Having gardens too close to your houses is not a wise move, because the water you use on them seeps down to your foundation and attracts termites. For those of us that have small yards or live in apartments or town-homes, container gardening might be the right choice.

It's a real time saver too!

In areas where there are very hot and dry summers, there can be drought, and potted plants don't require as much water as a full garden planted in the yard. In the North, you can utilize tropical plants. They can be pot and treated as summer specimens and then brought in for the winter. The same plants can remain outdoors all-year-round, where the climate is normally warm and sunny.

How to Plan Your Container Gardening

Planning Your Container Garden

Nothing beats the feeling of getting to use your herbs and vegetables, and even flowers, straight from your garden. There is a wide variety of plants that can be planted and grown in a container garden. With the right amount of planning, you can easily grow just about any type of plant you choose, given that their living conditions are met, of course.

- Plan which plants to grow. Plants have certain requirements that need to be met for them to grow properly. Therefore, you cannot just plant whichever plant you desire. You have to take into consideration the weather, climate and overall environment of where you live. Make a list of plants you want to grow and check their sun, water and soil requirements.

- Evaluate your house. Before you buy seeds or seedlings, carefully evaluate your home. Determine the areas which get the most sunlight, count how many hours the sunlight shines on those areas and identify the places which are partially shaded. Once you have listed those down, compare the requirements of the plants that you wish to grow and choose accordingly.
- Determine where to place the plants. If the area in your house which gets the most sun does not have enough space, choose to hang your containers or create shelves to place your plants on. These steps are very important, especially if you plan to expand your indoor garden in the future. You can also choose to set your plants somewhere else and then move them outside to get some sunlight; however, the constant moving may stress them out, which can hinder their growth.

Choosing the Containers: How to Choose the Right Pot for Every Plant

Picking the Right Containers

In truth, there is no specific or right container to use for container gardening. There are so many containers that you can choose to use. You can decide to use pots, old jugs or cartons or even watering cans. But to help you choose among hundreds of choices, here are some guidelines that you can follow.

- Style of the container. There are hundreds or even thousands of container styles. You can choose to use anything that you want at all. You can grow your plant in a clay pot, a fishbowl, in a shoebox or even in a trash can. Your choice will be depending on your budget, your design preference and the type of plant that you wish to grow.
- Size of the container. Of course, the larger the box, the higher the chance that your plants will grow healthy and strong. The advantage of using larger pots is that you need to water less frequently because the more soil there is, the longer the moisture will be held. However, if your space is limited, then you need to consider planting smaller plants that can survive in a limited space.

- Self-watering container. If you frequently travel or want a container garden but do not have that much time to tend to it, you can purchase a self-watering box to make sure that your plants get watered regularly. A self-watering container is very convenient to own. Still, if you live in an area where it mostly

rains, you might have to monitor your plants more closely to make sure that they do not drown and die.

- Drainage. As mentioned earlier, you can choose to use any container that you want. Still, you have to make sure that it has holes for drainage, or it is a material that you can easily make holes to.

Creating the Best Environment for Your Container Plants

Where will the container be located?

Light is one of the most important considerations if you want to grow happy, healthy, prolific flowers. Watch the sun and note if the container location is sunny, shady or partly shaded. Be sure to pick flowers that will thrive in that light.

Is this container going to be a centerpiece point or part of a grouping?

If this container is a stand-alone, "look at me" planting, it will need to be a large outstanding container planted with large foliage and flowers.If it's part of a grouping, you will have more leeway in choosing a variety of plants and containers. If you are planning on grouping your containers, apply the "rule of three." An odd number is always more pleasing when grouping anything, whether it's plants or containers.

What feeling am I trying to convey?

What type of home do you have? Is it stately and traditional? Homey and comfortable, a log cabin in the woods, or stucco home in a development?

The containers and flowers you choose should reflect that atmosphere. Look around at various containers in your area. Take photos with your phone while out walking. Look at gardening magazines and take note of the types of vessels and flowers used in areas similar to where you live.

Eventually, you will get a feel for what looks and feels right for you and your environment.

Where and When to Plant

Don't plant too early

Many people, even long time gardeners can plant too soon. Winter is gone, it is officially spring season, and everyone has cabin fever. Gardeners are ready to get out and grow! Make sure you know what zone you live in, and this will tell you when to expect the last frost. For most plants, cold is your enemy. By planting too early a late spring frost will destroy all of your hard work. It can be discouraging to make a great effort and then wake up and look out the window, and see everything covered with frost. Also, see below for a chart of when to grow based on soil conditions and frost times.

Your garden must be in an area that gets a lot of sunlight. Plants need the sun to photosynthesize, so planting away from the sun means slower growth and fewer crop yields. You want to plant where the daylight lasts for the day.

It may seems like common sense, but this is one of the main reasons why farmers do not yield enough crops. You must plan. Know what you want to plant seasons ahead and purchase the necessary seeds and tools to get the harvest started.

You can check online to see when your favorite fruits, veggies, nuts and herbs are in season. Waiting until that season comes to plant may mean that you won't yield the product you could have if you would have planned it before.

Scheduling is the key yet again when it comes to planting in this way. You must have your crops in the rotation when you are prepping for the year.

Organic agriculture reduces the use of non-renewable sources of energy. It means that you won't be wasting as much of the earth's resources by farming. Growing organic lessens the greenhouse effect and global warming, which is a major issue, especially for those of us who live in the northern hemisphere. It is only possible because growing organic stops carbon from seeping into the atmosphere while it's still in the soil. The increased carbon storage raises productivity because crops that are grown in carbon-rich soil tend to increase agriculture against climate change. It means that organic vegetables have a significantly better chance of surviving our rough climate than non-organic crops.

Make sure you choose the right plants for your location. You won't find papayas growing in most organic areas because the climate isn't right. You can learn which plants will thrive in your garden by checking the USDA's Hardiness Zones.

The Different Climatic Conditions across the American States

Over many centuries, plants have adapted to particular environmental conditions. They have grown accustomed to natural light sources and unlimited soil where their roots could spread. They have also been freely moved by wind. As a result, an average indoor environment is naturally hostile to most plants.

Even if a plant grows in a container, not all the natural conditions are present, unless the gardener provides them. Nevertheless, plants are adaptable even in hostile environments. They can struggle to keep living and growing. But, when the situation is close to nature, the plant could quickly respond by flowering and providing fruits and fragrance.

If the gardener provides adequate light, container, and soil, a lot of plants could do well in indoor settings.

Container gardening allows you to control the microenvironment of your garden. Several environmental factors will affect your container garden.

Light

Light and temperature are very important factors that can help you successfully grow plants in containers. The best thing about container gardening is that it offers convenience and portability. If you live in the temperate regions, the light conditions change, so make sure that you move your plants to get enough sunlight and avoid high temperatures.

Wind

The wind is considered a seasonal problem, and if your area suffers from strong winds during the summer, the containers may tumble over, especially if they are small. To prevent the wind from toppling over the pots, combine the weight of the box and soil to the upper portions of the plant for stable support. If your plants are blooming or have big leaves, and there is a strong wind – relocate them.

Heat Absorption

Too much heat can kill your plants. However, it is important to take note that the type of material of your pot can affect the heat absorption of your plant greatly.If you only have dark-colored plants, you can type Mediterranean plants, herbs and succulents that can withstand high heat temperature.

Seasonal Changes

Seasons can affect the growth of your container plants. The best thing about container gardening is that the changes in the season do not have a big impact on the plants as you can relocate your plants to different places in your house where they will be safe.

Choosing Plants

Choosing and growing your vegetables for your container garden is safer and healthier. You can be sure that no pesticide will harm you or your family. It is not hard to grow vegetables in containers as long as you know the right boxes to choose, the soil preparation, and the care and maintenance that you need to do.

For starters, you can try growing beans in a 12-inch wide container.

What to Grow In Your Garden

You can grow beets like a red ace, but make sure not to crowd the beets. Six plants in a 12-inch wide container should be enough.

Carrots have smaller varieties called short 'n sweet, little fingers, and Thumbelina. The smaller types only need six to eight inches deep containers to growth longer models may require deeper vessels.

Cauliflower, cabbage, broccoli, Brussels sprouts, kale, and other Cole crops can grow well in containers. They require big enough boxes, and won't grow well if you insist on using small containers.

Eggplant needs a five-gallon container to grow well. You also need to push a stake into the pot to provide proper support for the plant.

Lettuce and greens are the favorites of the most novice gardeners. They are not particular about the size of your container, although it is recommended to give them the proper spacing. Just sprinkle the seeds, keep the soil damp, and soon you will be harvesting fresh produce for your salad.

You can try radishes, cucumbers, spring onions, peppers, peas, squash, and others. You can buy your seedlings from a nursery or seeds from a garden supply shop.

Vegetables that are considered light lovers are beans, eggplant, pepper, and cucumber. Those that are okay with partial light are lettuce, carrot, spinach, broccoli, beets, peas, and collard greens.

Growing vegetables in containers will ensure that you and your family are eating the right kind of healthy food.

Seeds or Seedlings

You must predetermine if you should start planting the seeds outdoors or preparing them indoors in a controlled environment. That will depend on the type of plant you are growing, and the viable months left in your season. There is also the question of whether or not the seedling transplants well.

•Starting from **seeds** work if you are early into the season, and will plant veggies that mature into seedlings rather quickly (i.e., green peas, beans, summer squash, beets, carrots, corn, cucumbers, garlic, lettuce, parsnips, radishes, turnips, and watermelon).

•Cultivating **seedlings** indoors is best for pepper, any herbs, broccoli, Brussels sprouts, cabbage, cauliflower, celery, chard, eggplant, kale, leeks, onions, peppers, and tomatoes. These plants have slow maturation processes and can tolerate the disturbance of their roots during handling and transplanting.

When in doubt, look at the seed packaging and ask your local veggie shop proprietor.

A Special Type of Soil

In most cases, you seed your plants in another nutrient-rich mix of starter soil. You can buy this in small bags, or you can mix your own. The formula is simple, but you still need to buy the raw materials:

•4 parts compost (preferably screened)

•2 parts coir

•1 part vermiculite

•1 part perlite

For best results, mix now, leave alone for a few days, and then plant your seeds. BTW, there is no need to buy those particular types of seedling containers. I personally prefer to use old paper Mache egg trays laid on top of plastic egg trays. This way, even if the paper dissolves, you still have the plastic.

Toughen Up Young Sprouts!

If you are seeding indoors, you want to alter the seedlings to the outdoor environment before transplanting. That means placing the seedlings outdoors under indirect sunlight i.e., north facing. Bring the plants in when it gets too cold or too hot. After a couple of days hardening, the seedlings are good to go!

Easy Vegetables That Practically Grow Themselves

It's only natural. When you first start any project – and small-space gardening is no exception – you'd like to be successful at it. When you excel at something, then you want to keep doing it. So, you obviously would like to excel at your first attempt at growing vegetables, herbs and flowers. You're much more likely to adopt it as your hobby when you perform well.

Before you take a deep breath, thinking "boring!" look at these wonderfully diverse lists of the easiest vegetables to grow. There are more, but these lists will kick-start your thinking. And you're guaranteed to find many of your favorite foods.

1.Radishes

Radishes are easy to grow because they're practically pest-free. That eliminates much of the worry and maintenance that many experience with gardening. You can easily start this plant from seed at the beginning of the growing season and enjoy a zesty addition to your salads in the season. You'll want to choose from CHERRIETTE, Cherry Belle or Scarlet Globe for best results.

2.Carrots

Who can resist carrots? You will be amazed at your bountiful yield of carrots on your first gardening attempt. Few insects bother them, so they're low maintenance. You'll just want to use soil that isn't very rocky. While it won't affect the taste, rocky soil produces crooked carrots. A carrot is ready to harvest, by the way, as soon as the top breaks through the soil. The easiest varieties to grow are Scarlet Nantes, Danvers Half Long, and Sweet Treat.

3.Lettuce

You may have been told that this was difficult to grow. Don't believe it! It is one of the easiest vegetables for a novice gardener to plant successfully. Once you plant the seed the only thing you need to do is to watch it grow.

Don't limit your selection to merely leaf lettuce. Its vegetable comes in many varieties – all of which are delicious (and healthy!).Spinach is a type of lettuce, as is arugula. You may also want to try cultivating micro-greens. If you've never eaten these, you're in for a treat. They're tender greens that are at perfection when only a few weeks old.

4.Cucumbers

Yes, cucumbers! If you've ever seen these plants in a garden, then you know they're born to sprawl and spread. You only need to ensure that you give them plenty of room for their roots. If you do that, you'll be enjoying the crispness of fresh cucumbers right from your garden. Some of the best types for beginners to grow include Diva, Straight Eight and Salad Bush Hybrid.

5. Tomatoes

All you need for this plant to grow healthy and produce a crop is a good dependable water supply and sunlight. If you can deliver that, then you'll be enjoying tomatoes all summer – and probably sharing them with family and friends too!

Most gardeners don't start tomatoes from seeds but use what are called starter plants. You can buy these at your local nursery – even many home improvement stores carry them. If it's your first time growing tomatoes, try either the Big Boy or Roma variety.

6. Peppers

Peppers, specifically green bell peppers, are great for a beginning small-space gardener. The one fact you should know about it is its craving for warm temperatures. It's a slow grower, so don't be alarmed if it seems to "lag" your other crops in development. It is to be expected. The best time to harvest this vegetable is when the pepper is between three to four inches long and firm.

7. Beans

Think green beans. You even have some choices if you decide to plant this vegetable. Most grains are easy to grow. As a small-space gardener, you may also want to consider broad and pole beans. Broad beans are extremely easy to manage. As for the pole beans, the only issue you'll encounter is the need for a trellis for them to climb. But erecting a trellis is worth the little bit of extra effort if it means enjoying fresh beans.

8. Peas

A member of the legume family, the pea is a sure winner in a small-space garden. Choose from sweet or sugar beans; you can't go wrong with either.Both are nearly maintenance-free. And the only pest they attract is fruit flies. The good news is that these insects are easily controlled organically with NEEM oil. You might have heard of it. It's used by many as a natural repellent against mosquitoes that may be carrying the West Nile Virus.

You can begin planting these early as March, depending on where you live. There are only a few factors you'll want to consider. You'll want to make sure that if your pea plant grows tall, you provide a trellis or even a fence for it. If it's a shorter plant, make sure the container you place it in is deep. Harvest and enjoy!

9. Onions

Okay, I'll agree; onions are not the most glamorous vegetable you can grow. But it sure can add zing when you put it raw on a hamburger or other sandwiches. And it has a delicious sweet taste when SAUTEED. It enhances just about any meal. And if you're growing peppers as well – then you have yourself some fresh SAUTEED combination that can't be beaten. The only factor you need to consider is their love for the water.

How to Grow Any Plant

Now that you have your location, all of your supplies and your choices of fruits and vegetables you wish to grow, it is time to put it all together and start the planting process.

1. Start with the containers. Make a final check to ensure that the insides of each vessel are clean and free of debris. Also, closely inspect them for cracks. You want to find them now before you put them into use. Once you place your soil and plant in them, the increased weight and pressure will find these discrepancies for you.

2. And then, check your soil. It might sound simple, but make sure that you have more than enough for your containers. Leaving plants lying around, even in the shade, while you make a last-minute trip to the store puts them under stress.

3. Check for moisture. Soil needs to have the right consistency of moisture before you use it. While it does not require you to saturate it with water, it does mean is that it needs to contain more moisture than the bone-dry consistency that it presents when it is brought home in the bag. Using soil that is too dry will be hard to balance after planting. The roots will be feverishly searching the ground for any signs of moisture. Waiting until after it is planted will stress the plant. It will also be much more difficult to balance the moisture level throughout the soil after planting has occurred.

The best approach to moisturizing soil is to place the amount of dirt that you need in a bucket. Add a small amount of water to the ground and mix it until it is sufficiently damp. It means that it contains enough moisture that it is wet. Still, there should not be any patches where the soil is densely packed together because of a high concentration of water. Continue adding a small amount of water to the container until all of the ground is saturated.

4. Prep the plant. If you went with a seedling, your plant would already have a formed ball of soil packed around its root system. You mustn't try to pull this off.

Attempting to do so could easily damage the roots and jeopardize the health of the plant.

Your plant's root ball will also probably contain small round pellets. These pellets are fertilizer the grower has used and are not a reason for concern.

To transplant the seedling, you first need to inspect it. Take a good look at the soil surrounding the root ball. If it is rather dry, you will want to add some moisture to it before planting- even if you have moistened your soil in the container.

Place the seedling in a small container of water and allow it to absorb some of the water into the root ball. It doesn't need to float in water, or the soil surrounding the root ball will begin to loosen and break apart.

5. Move the plant. Once the seedling's root ball has received a sufficient amount of water, it can be transplanted into the new container. If the seedling's soil was sufficiently wet, then all that is necessary now is to transplant it from its original box to the new one. Since these seedlings are very delicate, you must take your time when removing them from their old container.

Even though most seedlings will be small, it is common for some people to pull them out of their old containers simply, which is the wrong thing to do. Drawing on the trunk of the seedling will cause it to snap in two or, at the very least, crack the vault of the plant, which could eventually kill it.

The preferred method of removal is to place the seedling's trunk between the second and third fingers of one hand and turn the container upside down. Grasp the bottom of the container with your free hand and gently shake it to loosen the seedling from its container. In some instances, the plant may be lodged in tightly, so it might become necessary to tap the bottom to move it.

The plant may still resist moving from the old container. If this occurs, take a butter knife and slide it around the inside of the vessel on all sides between it and the plant. It should free the seedling.

6. Inspect the root ball. Depending on how long the plant has been allowed to grow in its old container, it may have established quite an elaborate root system. There are times when you remove a plant, and all you will see is a twisted heap of roots with no visible soil. It means that the plant was allowed to remain in its container for far too long. While the plant can still be used, it will need some additional help to get started.

When roots are densely-packed together, you will need to separate and loosen them somewhat to allow them to get a head-start once they are placed in the new container.

If you leave them in a mangled mess, the plant will probably still grow, but it will take longer for the roots to realize that they are no longer constricted in a small place. Helping them speed up the process.

You will want to gently loosen the roots of the seedling by pulling them apart. Stay away from the base of the plant as you can easily pull roots off the plant base, injuring the plant. Pry the roots apart as much as you can and then plant.

If you see that the root ball is densely packed with soil, you can also help this situation by taking your butter knife and making some small incisions in different places in the ground to loosen it up. The marks do not have to be deep, and several small ones are much better for the plant than one or two large ones. Digging into the root ball too deep with a knife can damage roots deep down that you will not be able to see.

7. Plant your plants. Your new container should be filled with soil up to approximately one to one-and-half inches from the outer rim. Take your trowel or even your hand and remove a small amount of soil form the middle. Now, place the plant in the hole and pack the soil back around the plant while holding it upright.

You have to be very careful when packing soil around the plant as several things can happen. First, you may tend to push too hard around the plant in an attempt to seat it in the dirt firmly. In doing so, you can very snap off the plant at the ground or just below it. If you find that the plant isn't firm in the soil, gently remove the land and the plant and dig a slightly larger hole and try again. Never try to force the plant into the ground.

Second, is that you can end up with a plant that is buried too deep. You want the root system to be submerged, but not part of the trunk of the plant. Judge how high the soil needs to cover the plant.

Make sure that the plant is sitting straight so that there is less likely of a chance that it will tip over or grow at an angle. As it begins to produce vegetables, the added weight on one side could jeopardize the stability of the entire plant.

8. Watering. Surprisingly enough, this involves more than just dumping water on the plant. If water isn't distributed evenly, you take the chance that the plant will not receive valuable water in some parts of the soil. Since the plant has already been put under some stress through transplanting, it does not need the added importance of having to search for water, too.

When you water a new plant for the first time, the water is likely to drain through the soil very quickly since it has just been recently moved into the original container and hasn't had sufficient time to become packed. Even if the ground was moistened before the plant was planted, the soil still needs even more water to give the plant the best chance for survival.

If you dump water on the loose soil in the container, chances are very good that the land will become saturated, and the root ball will receive very little of the water. Why would this happen? Because the root ball is denser, and the water will be diverted to flow through the easy and loosing soil instead.

Instead of flooding the plant with a large volume of water all at once, a better approach is to give the plant a slow, steady drink so that it will allow it enough time to seep into every area—including the roots. It can be accomplished in some ways.

To complete your planting, you will probably have to add a little more soil to the container. When water is applied to the plant, it will automatically compact some of the lands on the surface, creating an indentation that needs to be filled. Some people also like to top off the surface surrounding the plant with mulch, sawdust, tree bark particles, landscape fabric or any assortment of other materials. It does not only help to keep precious water from evaporating, but it also serves as a barrier to help discourage the growth of weeds.

It is a good idea to label your plants with tags, so you know what varieties of each plant you are growing.

Growing Herbs

Grow your Herbs in Containers

Herbs can bring out the natural goodness of the food you eat. Most homemakers are not without potted herbs in their kitchen. The good thing about having fresh herbs in your kitchen is that you don't need to rush to a supermarket to get some in case you suddenly run out of your needed grass.

A good selection includes parsley, oregano, sage, rosemary, thyme, mint, basil, and chives.

Since most herbs like water, it is important to supply them with water all the time. However, there are also the so-called Mediterranean herbs that prefer soil that looks almost like sand. Mediterranean herbs include lavender, sage, rosemary, oregano, and thyme. Unlike most herbs, Mediterranean herbs will rot faster if the soil is too damp. You need to use pebbles or sand mulch around the said herbs.

The ideal place for your herbs is the kitchen. Just make sure to give your herbs the things they need most like sunlight and water.

Some herbs such as lemon balm, mints, and lemon verbena are invasive. Keeping them in containers can prevent them from causing trouble for other herbs in the garden.

You can choose to mix the herbs in a planter, but keep the invasive grasses in their respective containers to avoid taking over the space of other herbs.

Don't worry about frequent herb harvesting. Your herbs gain a lot of benefits from it. When you snip the tips off, the rest of the plant is somewhat stimulated to grow faster.

Getting your fresh supply of herbs from your garden most of (if not all) the time is not only cheap but also healthier.

How to Take Care of Your Herb Plants

Essential Care and Maintenance

After planting your preferred fruits, vegetables, and herbs, you need to observe proper maintenance and care. Taking care of your container garden is not difficult. Still, compared to a traditional garden, a container garden needs extra watering and feeding.

Watering

Most plants need frequent watering unless otherwise stated, as in the case of Mediterranean herbs. Potting soil quickly dries out, especially during windy or hot weather. You may need to water your plants more than once a day if the weather becomes unbelievably hot. In some cases, you may need to add liquid fertilizers, and you can use your watering can for that.

To check if your plant needs more water, insert your finger into the soil. If you feel that the land within the first few inches from the top is bone dry, then you need to water your plant. Make sure that your water penetrates the roots of your plant.

Applying Fertilizer

There is a need to fertilize your plants every two weeks to make sure that they get the right amount of nutrients. Liquid fertilizer is the easiest to use because you only need to mix the fertilizer with water and pour it onto the soil down to the roots. Organic fertilizer is a wise choice.

Beware of Pests

Although a container garden is less prone to pests than a traditional garden, there is still a chance that an infestation might happen. If you notice the presence of parasites, act immediately and remove possible sources of the pests. You can also apply NEEM oil on the leaves and stems of your plants to prevent the pests from invading your garden. The oil acts as a natural fungicide and pesticide. It also discourages the feeding of the pests.

Ample Sun Exposure

Plants need sunlight to thrive and grow, so make sure that your plants are getting the required amount of light. In the absence of natural light, you can use your artificial lighting that still makes photosynthesis possible.

Regular Pruning

Make your plants look fresh and alive all the time by pruning them. Dead leaves can make your plant look dull and unappealing, so you need to remove the dead leaves right away. Spray the leaves with water to remove the dust.

Plants with Disease

If you suspect that a certain plant in your garden has a disease, it is best to isolate the said plant and try to cure it. If the condition becomes worse, then it is best to discard the plant as well as its soil. Using the contaminated soil of the dead plant will only cause a problem.

Some Parting Words

It may take a while before you get used to container gardening. You need to exercise patience, diligence, discipline, perseverance, and willingness to learn and discover new things. Your container garden may not look appealing now, but understand that you have just begun. Your passion and your container garden need some time to bloom into something more radiant and beautiful. Be patient so that you will reap your reward.

How to Protect Your Plants

Containers that have once been rich in color and foliage tend to fade and fail, gradually becoming worn out as the midsummer begins to roll in. As the temperatures start to rise, pretty blossoms and fleshy leaves start to wither and disappear. Fortunately, with proper care, your containers can flourish with vibrant health all summer.

There are crucial steps below that can be taken to create and maintain a brilliant display all through summer:

•The first step towards having a healthy container is selecting the correct size of the pot, which is determined by different factors. Choosing a small planter with crowded roots will result in less water, oxygen, and nutrients available to the roots, and all these are important for their healthy growth.

•On the other hand, when containers are too big, they will result in having excess moisture in the soil, thereby cutting off oxygen and eventually drowning the roots. Also, planters that have too much space with moist soil will help in solving most plant problems.

•In a situation where the recommended spacing is ten to twelve inches, for example, you will make sure the plants are about six to eight inches apart. Generally, if their average growth is about ten to 12 inches tall, you should opt for a pot that is nearly half the size or width of around six to eight inches. In the case of plants that grow between 24 to 36 inches tall, you will need a larger container of about 24 inches in diameter. Also, ensure your pot is composed of drainage holes with the required material below it to enable excess water are flowing out smoothly.

•It is also advisable to invert a smaller plastic pot over the drainage holes if adding more weight is an issue. There has also been some controversy as regards styrene from Styrofoam leeching into edibles. It was concluded that the low levels of styrene that are found in packaged food are due to the leaching that comes from the

37

polystyrene containers in which they were packed. It is therefore recommended to make use of gravel, pieces of broken pottery, pebbles, nutshells, sticks, pinecones, or coffees as your drainage.

•Also, note that container plants don't like their roots sitting in water. It will result in a wet root environment that will cause most bedding plants to sulk and have low growth. They can also cause the roots to rot, which makes planters inconvenient.

•Drainage is also required to help provide your potted roots with adequate aeration. Because without this, and it will be hard for them to breathe and get easy access to oxygen.

Keeping the Bugs Out and How to Get Rid Of Bugs Naturally

Managing Pests and Plant Diseases

There are different natural and organic ways of dealing with pest and disease issues in the garden, most of which have been proved useful over recent years. In modern times, most of these techniques are usually referred to as Integrated Pest Management (IPM). They can also be related to Organic Pest Management (OPM).

For effective pest and plant disease management, close observation of your garden more often is the fundamental way to start. The ability to recognize in time that your plant is stressed will allow you to take proactive steps to help keep these pests and plant diseases in check. Nevertheless, leaving these pests and diseases unchecked will only result in an unhealthy garden with an unhealthy environment.

To help discourage these garden pests and diseases from causing damage to your garden, without having to use synthetic, non-organic controls, you are advised to consider the following techniques.

38

•Make sure you choose the best site and soil for the type of plants you are growing. And it will go a long way in reducing plant stress and its vulnerability to diseases and pests. If you expose your plants to excessive or too little sun, shade, fertilizer, or water, they can be stressed up. You are advised to make use of aged compost to help provide your plants with all the nutrients they need.

•You are advised to choose plant species or varieties that are resistant. Make sure you check your seed packets, including the plant labels for the pest and diseases, as well as resistance. Always try to mix different plant families to create diversity. It is useful in preventing the rapid spread of pests and plant diseases that are known for attacking specific plant groups.

•Engage in pruning or pinching to help in removing damaged or diseased leaves with branches. And it will also help in increasing the light as well as air circulation in your garden.

•You can and-pick insect pests off the plants in your container garden. You can get insects such as snails, slugs, giant adult insects, caterpillars. You can easily handpick and drop them off into soapy water.

•Make use of lures to get insects trapped using both olfactory and visual. For instance, making use of yellow sticky boards can help control whiteflies, cucumber beetles, THRIPS, and cabbage worms.

•You can make use of pest barricades such as sticky bands or floating row covers to get the pests off the plants and planting beds.

•Invite beneficial insects to your container garden. Examples of these beneficial insects include lacewings, lady beetles, and spine soldier beetles. You can also grow plants that will provide nectar and pollen for beneficial insects.

•Always keep your container garden free from plant debris. Remember that pest insects are capable of hiding or finding shelter in dropped or dead leaves. Get the soil turned during the fall or in between plantings to help expose these hidden pests.

•Bacteria, viruses, or fungi can be engaged to help kill some of these pests and garden diseases. Bacillus THURINGIENSIS is commonly used, and it is a bacteria species that gives out toxins that are poisonous to most insect pests.

•Finally, some pests and plant diseases can be controlled with the use of non-toxic sprays, such as a forceful spray of water with the garden hose to dislodge them effectively.

Ideas to Make Beautiful Containers Gardening
Fun ways to make and decorate containers with kids

Finding boxes can be a lot of fun. They can be painted and decorated and it could be a great activity for kids too, who will enjoy making excellent pots out of everyday things.

Look in your garage for things you can use. Look around your house. Try to find unusual objects to use in the garden. Almost anything can be a planter! The more unique it is, the funnier it will be.

There are many ways you can decorate containers; you can paint them, you can attach cool things to them, you can draw on them and you can build them out of different materials. Let's look at some different ways you can decorate your containers.

Painting

You can use tempera paints on many different materials to make them beautiful. You can free paint on your containers. You can paint each box a different color, or you can paint them all the same color. You can paint abstract shapes on the containers. You can paint rainbows or polka dots. You can paint a scene in the garden. You can paint pictures of the people who work in the garden. You can paint pictures of the vegetables growing in each container, which is also an excellent way to remember what you are growingin each box! You can paint your containers however you like - there is no wrong way to do it!

Stencils

You can use stencils to make patterns on the containers. To make a simple stencil, draw a star or other dull object on a manila file folder. Then place the stencil against the box and fill it in with paint. You can also use spray paint to do this quickly. One stencil can be used to decorate an entire container with lots of stars! What other shapes can you think of that would be excellent stencils?

Drawing

Just like painting, you can use permanent markers to draw on your containers. If your box is too dark for drawing, you can spray paint it white first. You can also paint it another light color. Then, you can draw on it, or write your name on it, or write an explanation of what is in the pot. You can even write what kind of plant it is, and how to take care for it!

Found objects

You can look around your house and garden to find objects to attach to the containers. If you do this, be sure to paint over them with clear lacquer. Lacquer will seal the images in and protect them from the rain. Have a grownup help you with this part. Try to think of other neat things you can glue to your containers.

Of course, each container can be a combination of these techniques. For instance, you might want to paint or draw a scene of a garden on your vessel. You can make a stencil in the shape of corn plants to add them to the stage. Then you could glue a picture of yourself in the garden, and glue dried beans to show the bean plant! Be creative and think of ways you can mix and match the different ways to decorate your container.

Building containers

You can also build neat boxes from various materials. When you do so, be sure to think creatively about how they will look as well as how they will work. Artists call thinking this way, combining *form* and *function*. The structure is how the container looks and service is how it works. If you approach your content creation with form and function in mind, you will have a serene looking container garden that works well!

Making Containers from Recycled Materials

Cut the bottom off a milk jug. Turn the jug upside down. Then, thread a seedling that is at least four or five inches tall through the top of the jar. Be sure to keep the seedling in its root ball when you do this. Fill the rest of the jug at least halfway with soil. Punch holes in the sides of the jar at least four inches from the bottom. You can reinforce the holes with grommets. Make at least three holes, so the jug is balanced. Then, attach ropes or twine to the pits and hang the jar. Water normally. You can also make larger upside-down pots from buckets. As always, be creative!

Another kind of container is called a grow bag. It is what it sounds like: a bag for growing vegetables! You can buy grow bags at garden supply stores or make your own. The easiest way to make a grow bag is with a reusable shopping bag. These bags will hold their form and should not fall over. The shopping bag is porous so that air will reach the roots, and water will drain quickly. Because water flows so smoothly, be sure to check the container at least once a day to make sure it does not dry out. An extra advantage of using a shopping bag is that it has handled - so you can move it around quickly! Be sure to use a sturdy material like canvas. Cheap reusable bags may tear from the weight of the soil. Grow bags are best for growing small or medium-sized vegetables like tomatoes and peppers.

Creative containers

Let's get creative with our containers. Anything can be a container. Look around - you can find boxes everywhere that you can use in your garden!

Once you have decided what you are going to plant, you need to find out what size containers you need. Make a list of the vegetables you will grow. Then make a list of boxes. Your listing should say whether the containers you need are small, medium, or large. Once you know how many of each kind you need, start looking!

Very small plants do not need much room to grow and thrive. For these plants, like lettuce, radishes or carrots, small containers will do. You can use coffee cans with holes punched in the bottom. Or you can cut the tops off of milk jugs. Keep reading for more ideas about what you can use to make containers.

Anything can be a container if it is sturdy, holds water, and can be drained. What that means is that the walls should be strong enough to hold a lot of wet soil, which is cumbersome. It should also not leak through the sides. And it can be drained if you can make holes in the bottom of it. That means that glass or solid concrete containers do not work well. If the box does not drain, the plant will not grow properly.

If you are using containers with a porous material, they might need to be lined. "Porous" materials have tiny holes in them and can absorb water. Wood is an example of a porous material. If the wood is soaked in water, it will absorb it. It will make the wood soft and rotten over time, which will ruin your container. You can find out if a material is porous by pouring water on it. If you can wipe all of the water off with a cloth, it is not porous. If you wipe it off and the material stays wet, it is probably porous.

Some materials, like terra cotta, are porous but are not damaged by becoming wet. Still, they can have leftover minerals or even plant diseases in them. If you buy used terra cotta pots, be sure to clean them before you use them. You can kill any infections in them by baking them at 225 F for an hour. Be sure to open the windows while you do this, as it can get smelly!

You can line wooden containers with plastic sheets or garbage bags. Poke holes in the bottom of the plastic so that water can drain. Terra cotta pots do not have to be lined. If you choose to do so, you can use plastic pot liners that are made just for this purpose.

You can also buy upside-down containers for growing vegetables like tomatoes or peppers. These are fun to grow in. They are also more relaxed. Upside-down plants do not need stakes or cages to hold them up. Pests have a hard time finding upside-down planters. You can buy upside-down planters that come with everything you need at the garden store. Or you can make your own out of milk jugs.

Toxic materials

Please make sure not to use containers with toxic materials for your boxes. Water and soil can leach poisonous substances right into your plants. Some stuff we do not apply for containers is treated wood, old barrels that carried toxic chemicals, certain art supplies, and any box that might contain a poisonous residue. If in doubt, don't use it!

Tips and Tricks for Container Gardening

Container gardening is less expensive than maintaining a regular garden; however, it can still cost you a lot. By merely planning how you would go about with your container gardening, you could cut the cost by half. How do you do this?

Tips on How to Reduce Container Gardening Costs

Tips When Setting a Budget

Assess why you are into container gardening. It is the foundation of your garden. If your motive is to earn, then you can plan the plants that you are going to have, the materials that you would need and other pertinent data. However, if you have no solid reasons why you are into this, you would just do things without regard to the future, and you might spend unnecessarily. If you have finally decided why you are bent on having container gardening, then you can do smart planning.

Write down your plans. You would see the overall picture when you write down your thoughts, strategies, ideas and blueprint of your garden. You would also be able to list down all the things you would need when you have a picture of your plans and not just a mental image. Plus, you could estimate the timeframe you need to complete your garden.

Make a to-buy list ahead of time and keep an eye on the costs. You can check how much you would need when you plan your garden needs. You could do your shopping at the end of the season sales and save money. Buy the items and supplies that you need throughout the year and store them until they are required. When you do not know the things you need for the whole year, you tend to buy them according to the time you need them, and that could be costly for you.

Study how you would go about your plans. You can ask the opinions of other garden experts or enthusiasts or ask for help from friends or other people you know who are into container gardening. You could adjust your plans when you acquire better suggestions or ideas.

Thorough planning would save you money and cause you to spend less than necessary for your container gardening.

10 Tips to lessen your container gardening expenses

Start from seeds.

Most seeds cost less than a dollar. If you would start from scratch, it may take some time and more effort, but you would save a lot. As you go looking for seeds for your container garden, you might find be confused with some of the terms used for describing seeds. For your clarification:

- F1 varieties or hybrids. It is the expensive seeds as the process of producing these seeds is more complicated than usual. The crossing of two-parent varieties is done so that a new one will be created.
- Genetically modified. These seeds are created in the laboratories where their genes are manipulated.
- Open-pollinated varieties. Also known as heirloom varieties, these seeds can be reused year after year. They are found to be more resistant to various crop diseases.
- Organic seed. Grown without the use of pesticides, fungicides, herbicides, or fertilizers.

For newbies, choose the "easy seeds" to plant. These are hardy and easy to plant, plus they grow earlier, too.

Buy seedlings.

Having healthy, young plants also cost less in the long run. They have a higher probability of surviving than seeds. Lesser efforts are required to ensure that they survive the transfer to another occasion. When buying seedlings, make sure to check the leaves; they should be green, and if there are patches of white or dried leaves, avoid these plants as they could mean weak or unhealthy plants. They may not last long when you transplant them. Check also if they are firmly attached to a group. Trying to separate and plant them could cause trauma to the plant and cause its death. Those planted singly are easier to transplant and have a higher probability of surviving a transplant. Also, do not just depend on the height of the plants to determine if they can survive. It has been noticed that smaller plants do better at staying alive when transplanted.

Buy all your garden needs during the sale.

It usually takes place every end of the growing season. At this time, containers are marked down at half prices. Even other supplies such as tools and decorative supplies would cost less. Therefore, if you have any garden need that can wait until the clearance sales, acquire them during that time and save money.

Propagate your seedlings.

Some seedlings are effortless to propagate. Instead of buying many of these plants, just be the one to multiply them and save money. Look for plants that can be spread only by simply cutting branches and putting them in water. When roots start to come from those branches, plant them in containers or pots. There is even something better than this. Some plants just propagate on-their-own. All you have to do is to transplant them when they are strong enough to be transferred to a different container from the mother plant.

Recycle.

Instead of buying containers, take a closer look at things in your house. Maybe there are old pails that you can use as pots. Old baskets can be redecorated and be used as vases in your container gardening. Be creative and imaginative and transform those old buckets or bottles into something useful. You would discover that there are many things in your house (specifically in your attic or basement) that can be recycled and converted into garden items.

Exchange seeds or seedlings with others.

Instead of looking and buying seeds and seedlings from garden centers, contact friends who are garden container enthusiasts and strike a deal with them. You can trade seeds and seedlings. You would not have to spend money at all, plus that is also building camaraderie with other gardeners.

Make your compost.

Instead of buying fertilizers, you can make your compost in your backyard. Simply dig a small portion, and leftovers and other biodegradable things can be placed there. Not only have you saved money for fertilizer or compost, but you have also helped the environment by cutting the garbage being sent to landfills.

Compare and contrast prices.

You can save money when you try to check different stores, flea markets, yard sales, and thrift stores. Sometimes, one tends to patronize a specific store, and he or she misses other great deals at different stores. You can also check online for the most significant sales and best offers of different shops. Look for coupons or vouchers too in your daily newspapers.

Choose edible plants.

Instead of buying exotic and expensive plants, be practical and buy things that you could use in your kitchen. You do not only save money on caring for those strange plants, but you also save grocery money when you harvest your vegetables or herbs in your container garden. Think of all the herbs and vegetables that you always need in your kitchen like garlic, ginger, parsley or celery and plant them. Whenever you need any of these, you do not have to shell out cash. Just go to your garden and harvest from them. Plus, this might motivate you to start a little business and increase your income all the more. Neighbors or friends could just order some of your products instead of buying them in the local grocery stores. You could also try edible flowers. That way, you have house décor and ingredients for dishes at the same time.

Place an ad, use your social media accounts or the word of mouth advertisement and just inform other people that you are into container gardening.

You would be amazed at how sometimes people just offer many tips, items or even plants for you, for free. For some people, instead of having tools or gardening supplies that are not being used in their homes or just adding spaces in their garage or sheds, they would instead give them to other garden enthusiasts if they know they require those. You save money, and at the same time, you have helped those people dispose of the items they consider as junk in their homes.

One does not need to spend so much. Be wise and use these tips and see how much you can save by doing so.

Preparing Your Tools and Supplies

After you have decided and researched what you will grow in your container garden, the following step would be to collect the gardening tools the supplies that you will need. Once you have done that, you will then move on to preparing all of your containers.

Gardening Tools and Supplies

You will need some essential tools and planting materials to make the maintenance and care of your container garden a pleasant and productive experience.

At a garden center, purchase planting bagged planting materials, including topsoil, organic mulch and compost. These are usually sold in volume or cubic feet. Use an online calculator for gardeners to find out how much you will need. Most calculators will require you to type in the dimensions of your gardening area and how dense you want your planting material to be.

Since you will be working with a container garden, you are going to need hand tools for gardening. Aim for quality, since most devices are well worth the price. The necessary tools that you will need to start with are a pair of gardening gloves. A watering can, a small trowel or a three-pronged fork, and a compost scoop.

If you want to build up your gardening tool collection, consider the following: secateurs (a specific pair of scissors for trimming and pruning), a dibber (to create more precise holes for your seeds), and a soil sieve. You should also have a dustpan and brush to sweep up soil that gets spilled over your containers.

Garden Center Shopping Tips

You can get your seeds or seedlings at a local farmers' market or nursery. There will be a wide array of vegetable choices, so make sure to bring a list of the ones you have selected to avoid feeling overwhelmed.

In choosing seedlings, check the textures, leaf colors and the roots. Avoid plants that have brown or notched leaf edges, papery, bleached leaves, and too many scars and broken stems. Also, check the care tags to verify if the seedlings can grow with other plants in the same container.

It is advised that you visit the nursery on a weekday so that the salesperson will be able to accommodate you better and answer all of your questions. Frequently, the plants are organized based on the conditions that enable them to grow well, such as "sunny or dry" and "shade tolerant." Choose the appropriate ones based on your available area.

Prepare your Containers

Before planting your seedlings and seeds, you will need to prepare your potting mix. The first step is to make sure that all of the containers are clean and free from any contaminants that might harm your plants, such as insect repellent spray. Check the drainage holes to see if there is enough to prevent the soil from getting soaked. You do not have to place gravel or pot shards in the bottom of the containers; instead, set a layer of newspaper to prevent the potting mix from spilling. If your receptacle is too deep, one way to minimize the amount of potting mix that you will use is to place some gravel in the bottom.

Make sure to prepare your potting mix outdoors as potting soil can irritate your lungs, skin and eyes.

Do not use plain garden soil for your container garden, as this is too dense. Instead, mix houseplant soil mixture with your loamy soil. There are plenty of commercial planting mixes available at garden centers. You can also come up with your mix at home by combining compost with pulverized perlite, vermiculite, pine or fir bark. For every cubic foot of mix, include (4 Oz) of dolomitic limestone, (4 Oz) of greensand, (2 Oz) of blood meal, (1 lb.) of rock phosphate or colloidal phosphate, and (1 lb.) of granite dust. As you fill up each container, leave at least 1 inch of space between the surface of the soil and the rim of the box so that you can leave room for watering.

After you have mixed the potting soil, the following step is to pre-moisten it by watering it several times and then mixing it some more. The soil should be consistently moist before you start planting.

Tips for Starting Seeds

Depending on the type and quality of the seeds you're trying to get started, starting your seeds can be a rewarding experience, or it can be frustrating to the point of tears. It's exhilarating to check on your seeds to find they've sprouted overnight, and there's nothing better than watching a seed you've sprouted grow into a mature plant complete with tasty vegetables. On the other hand, sometimes you can do everything in your power to bring your seeds to life, only to have them not sprout or sprout, but fail to grow into healthy plants.

Seeds should be started according to the manufacturer's instructions. These instructions are usually found on the seed packet and are often the best way to give your seeds a great shot at life. After all, it benefits a manufacturer when you're able to get their grains to grow because you're likely to purchase from them again in the future.

To get up and to run, your seeds need three things:

• Healthy soil.

• Water.

• Light.

Although one could reasonably surmise seeds should be able to sprout in any soil since they're designed to propagate naturally, having the right soil blend will give your seedlings a better shot at life. While the perfect soil blend is dependent on the type of seed being planted, the following mix works well for most seed types:

• 4 parts perlite.

• 4 parts sphagnum moss.

• 1 part worm castings.

If worm castings aren't available, you can use equal parts perlite and sphagnum moss to good effect. Seedlings do best in soil that hasn't had fertilizer added. You can add it if you want, but wait until they get their second set of leaves. Most seedlings grow best when the soil temperature is kept between 65 and 70 degrees F.

In addition to good soil, your seeds are going to need light, and lots of it.

If you're starting your seeds indoors, the ambient light in the house probably isn't going to be enough. You can set up a small artificial lighting system to make sure your plants get the view they need. Use a combination of fresh and warm fluorescent bulbs and set them on a timer, so your plants get at least 14 hours of light a day. The lights need to be set up, so they're only a few inches away from the plants.

Follow the planting instruction on the seed packet when setting your seeds in the soil. Some seeds are supposed to be broadcast onto the surface of the land. Some need to be placed just below the surface, while others do best when placed an inch or more into the ground. Some seeds need to be oriented in a specific direction to ensure proper growth.

After planting your seeds, you need to keep the soil around them damp, but not soaking wet. Moist, well-drained soil is conducive to seed-starting. Let your soil dry out, and you're going to reduce the number of seeds that sprout drastically. It is problematic because the small pots that seeds are typically started in are tough to keep moist, especially if they're being kept under warm lights. If you're like me and tend to forget to water your plants, a self-watering system can be a lifesaver. These systems take the guesswork out of watering because they water your plants for you and will keep your seeds beautiful and damp the way they need to be to sprout.

If you're using tap water to water your plants, let the water warm up to room temperature before using it. Don't use water that's passed through a water softener because it will contain too much sodium. Chlorinated water needs to be left out overnight to get rid of the chlorine.

Plants that are started outside tend to be healthier because they're exposed to the elements from an early age. They're forced to develop stronger roots and a thicker stem to withstand the wind. You can simulate this effect indoors by setting up a fan in your grow area and letting it blow a gentle breeze across your seedlings for a few hours a day.

Some plants don't lend themselves well to being transplanted, and their seeds have to be started in the containers in which they're going to be grown.

When you're using smaller containers, this isn't a problem because you can bring the boxes inside to get the seeds started. When planting in larger vessels that aren't mobile, you may have to start your seeds outdoors. Make sure you follow the manufacturer's recommendations and avoid planting your seeds too early. If your seeds are exposed to excessively cold weather while germinating, they may not sprout. If they do germinate, the seedlings will be stressed out and probably won't grow into healthy plants.

Damping Off

Amongst the issues that can crop up and affect seedling growth, damping off is the most prevalent. It is a disease brought about by the growth of fungus that can cause stop germination dead in its tracks and can kill off seedlings in a hurry. Damping-off can kill seeds before they emerge from the ground, or it can kill young seedlings after they sprout.

The following symptoms are indicative of damping-off:

• Dying seedlings.

• Leaf spotting.

• Mold on the surface of your soil.

• Rotting roots.

- Seedlings that turns black.

- Seeds that won't sprout.

- Thin seedlings.

- Thin stems.

- Wiry seedlings.

Several fungi types can cause damping off. These fungi live in the ground and can start growing and attacking your plants if conditions are right. Damping-off usually takes place in localized patches and spreads outward in a circle. If you notice some of your seedlings are dying off, getting rid of the tray that's damping off can stop the disease from spreading.

The best way to prevent damping off is to use clean soil from trusted sources. Sterilize your containers before use and keep your seed trays in a clean, sterile area. Don't use the same gloves and tools on your seedlings that you use in your garden because you risk introducing new fungi to your soil.

Unless you're using sterilized soil, there will always be some fungi in your soil. It isn't necessarily a bad thing, as long as you're able to keep the bad mushrooms in check. You can do this by using soil that drains well and doesn't hold too much water. There's a fine line between keeping your soil damp and saturating it with water. Cross the front, and you're creating conditions conducive to the growth of the harmful fungus that causes damping off.

Vigorous seedlings and plants will be less susceptible to fungi, so be sure to give your plants what they need to overgrow. Make sure soil temperatures are correct, give them the exact amount of light and make sure they get the water they need, but no more than what's necessary. Damping-off is no longer a concern once plants make it through the seedling stage and mature into adult plants.

Harvesting and Storing Your Crop

The most enjoyable part of container gardening starts when the fruit has ripened, and it is time to harvest the crop. It is the time when you sample your produce as you are watering and enjoy the benefits of all your hard work.

Root vegetables are easy to harvest; just pull them up, cut off the leaves and prepare the plant! If you have used the soil mix, then it is easy to pull up your root vegetables with no digging. These will typically be okay in the ground for several weeks once ripe, meaning you can pull them up as and when you need them rather than removing all at once.

With your other plants, the fruits are likely to be ready at different times. Typically with tomatoes, for example, the fruits are not all ripe on the same day. They ripen over time, so you have to check the plants and remove the ripe fruit before they go past their best. Be careful how you delete them as pulling at the plant could damage it and introduce disease.

Any vegetable that grows on a stalk can either be removed by cutting with scissors or a knife (very carefully) or pinching it between your finger and nails. You need a clean cut so that you do not introduce infection into your plant.

Once your vegetables are overripe, the taste can start to deteriorate; tomatoes become squishy, root vegetables grow woody and so on. You need to keep an eye on your veggies, so they do not go past their best.

Harvest Your Crop When You Will Use It

You should only harvest your vegetables when you are going to use them or if you are going to use them in the following day or two as most home-grown produce, particularly soft vegetables, do not store well. It is because they are not covered in the chemicals that are used by the commercial growers to preserve them. Your crop will stay fresher longer on the plants or in the ground than they will, in general, in your refrigerator.

However, should you have vegetables that are going past their prime, then you will need to harvest them and either stores them or make something from them; otherwise, they can rot on the plants or attract unwanted pests.

There are lots of dishes you can make with your excess produce, and you can certainly enjoy a few weeks of delicious cooking from the fruits of your labor.

Freeze Your Excess Produce

Most other vegetables can be frozen, with potatoes being one of the main exceptions. Potatoes can be stored for several months in paper bags in a cool dark place. Onions can be cooked and frozen though they too will store in a cool dark place for many months if dried and hung. Grow enough of these, and they can easily supply you through the winter months.

Vegetables can be frozen by blanching them to remove bacteria and then plunging them into icy cold water to stop the cooking process. These can be put into portion-sized containers and frozen as a "lump," or you can spread them on trays, freeze them and then bag them up afterward. Most vegetables only need blanching for 30 to 60 seconds with harder plants needing longer blanching times than softer ones.

Be Creative with Your Excess Produce

Of course, there is much more you can do with your crop other than just freeze it. Some people will prepare meals with their products and freeze the meals, or you can make jams, chutneys, sauces or pickles, depending on what you have an excess.

If I have too many tomatoes, then I tend to make either tomato ketchup, tomato soup or tomato sauce for pasta. When I have an excess of root vegetables, I will usually make a massive batch of stew and then freeze the finished product in portion-sized containers for quick ready meals. Fruits like strawberries get turned in to jams, and my herbs are dried and stored in boxes for use throughout the year.

If you are adventurous, then many fruits and vegetables that you grow at home can be made into wine, which is an interesting alternative use for a bumper harvest

If you do not have the time to do anything with your excess crop, you are bound to have friends, family and neighbors who would be more than happy to receive your excess fresh produce. If you prefer, you could even donate them to a soup kitchen or food bank.

Just remember to be careful to avoid damaging your plants when harvesting the crop. If the frosts are coming, you will need to collect whatever is left of your vegetables, so they do not get damaged. You can store your plants or use them to make dishes that are then frozen or preserved for enjoyment during the winter months.

Drying and Preserving Herbs

Harvesting herbs is one of the best moments in gardening. It is when you get to appreciate all your efforts and patience for gardening. However, you can't use all of these herbs at the same time, and you can't delay harvesting it either. Some herbs need to be entirely uprooted to be collected while you have to pick out all the flowers and leaves of some. Otherwise, they will no longer be as fresh and tasty when used for cooking.

That's why you must learn how to preserve herbs. Preserved herbs last longer and can be stored and used all year round. Preserving herbs usually includes drying, freezing, dehydrating or mixing them in oil.

These preservation methods are relatively easy and do not require the use of complicated tools and materials. All the materials you'll need can be found in your kitchen. Here's how you can preserve your herbs.

1. Harvesting – before you preserve your herbs, you need to harvest the edible parts of the plant. Take scissors or a knife and use it to cut the stems, leaves or flowers of the herb. After collecting the herbs, wash it with water. Gently spray it with water and let it dry by patting it with a paper towel or napkin. It's best to immediately proceed with preserving the herbs to maintain the shape and color of the herbs.

2. Maintain the Appearance – some herbs change appearance when preserved. It changes its color, its shape and size. However, some herbs can retain their appearance:

a. Herbs with sharp leaves are more natural to preserve since the sheets do not deform easily. They can maintain their color and shape. Some good examples are rosemary, thyme and sage.

b. Herbs with tender and soft leaves are a bit trickier since the leaves can change shape, size and color. Herbs like parsley, basil and mint fall under this category.

Some herbs are better used fresh than dried, but trial and error is the best way to determine which herbs you'll preserve. After all, you might find a specific herb better used when preserved than when it is fresh. Personal preferences will also affect your decision when it comes to choosing which herbs you'll maintain.

3. Drying – this is the most common and popular method of preserving herbs. There are several ways to dry herbs. Some of the methods are hanging, towel drying, air drying, outdoor drying, drying using a microwave or oven, natural drying, drying through the use of desiccants and drying by pressing.

4. Hanging – this involved hanging the herbs in a dark area. Its method is also used in preserving flowers like roses. It will take a couple of days before the herbs are completely dried up. To do this, take the herbs you wish to dry and tie them in groups. Attach a string around the stems. Its line must be long enough to hang the herbs upside down. Take the herbs and hang them in a relaxed and dark area like a closet or kitchen cabinet. Make sure that the wardrobe and offices are clean and free of pests and insects to avoid damages. Check after a couple of days. The leaves should be dry with a brittle texture.

5. Towel Drying – take the herbs and a clean towel. Place the sheet on a clean and flat surface. After washing and cleaning the herbs, lay the herbs on the cloth. Do not overcrowd the herbs on one towel. It works best when there's enough space between each herb. Set aside and leave the herbs on the sheet until completely dry.

6. Air Drying – similar to hanging, but except for a closet. Take the herbs and tie them in bundles and groups. Make sure that each package is of the same herb variety and size. Make sure to hang the herbs upside down, with the flowers and leaves facing downwards. It will help in drying all the moisture in the grass. Put the herbs in separate paper bags and secure the end with a string. The paper bag speeds up the drying process and, at the same time, catches falling leaves, flowers or seeds which you can use in the future. Hang the herbs and remove them when they are dehydrated.

7. Outdoor Drying –take the herbs and tie them in bundles. Put them inside a paper bag and secure the ends. The paper bag will prevent the herbs from being too dried up, which can cause the herbs to lose their flavor. Then, hang the herbs outside where there is direct sunlight. Its method is perfect for drying herbs intended for craft and DIY projects.

8. Drying Using an Oven or Microwave – if you don't have the patience of waiting for days for the herbs to dry, you can use an oven or microwave to speed up the drying process. Take the herbs and place them on a rack lined with baking paper. Make sure that the herbs do not touch each other. Put them inside the oven or microwave and set it on the lowest setting possible. Dry in the oven or microwave for about a minute. After that, take the herbs and check if they're dried completely. If not, add another 30 seconds. Once the herbs are dried, store them for future use.

9. Natural Drying – natural drying allows the herbs to dry in a container. Though this is not the best way to dry herbs, it works well with rosemary and fennel. Take the herbs and place them in a box. Arrange the herbs properly and leave the container in a warm and dry place. Check regularly and monitor for any signs of damages like mildew.

10. Use of Desiccant – desiccant are substances that drain moisture from an object. A good example would be silica gel, sand and borax. Take the herbs, the desiccant and a bowl. Cover the base of the container with desiccant and place the herbs on it. After that, add another layer of desiccant on the grass. Set aside and check once in a while to see if the herbs are already dry.

11. Pressing – simply take the herbs and place them between pages of note. Close the text and add some weight on top of it. After a few days, the herbs are pressed and dried. It is perfect for crafts and artworks.

12. Freezing – another method of preserving herbs is by freezing. Its process works best with herbs with soft and tender leaves like basil, mint and lemon balm. Take the herbs and wash them thoroughly. Boil some water and dip the herbs to blanch them. Afterward, put the herbs straight into ice-cold water and freeze. Blanching your herbs will help them last up to six months.

13. Preserve in Oil – use natural and organic oil in preserving the herbs. The most suitable oil is olive oil. Take the herbs and wash them thoroughly. Pat dry with a paper towel and put it inside a jar. Pour oil into the pot, making sure that all the herbs are covered and submerged in oil. Secure the jar and refrigerate.

These methods are effortless and easy to follow. Aside from that, preserving helps in retaining the original color and flavor of the herbs. Just make sure to wash the herbs thoroughly before preserving them. Remove damaged leaves or flowers. Cut the herbs in the same length and sizes and always group them with their variety. It's also recommended that you have separate jars for each type of preserved herbs.

Herb Gardening

When planting herbs at home, there are important tips that will help you achieve success even without experience in gardening. Some of these tips include;

Tip #1: Determine the herbs that you would like to plant starting with the simplest trio of basil, rosemary and oregano or chives.

Tip #2: Ensure that you do your gardening in a suitable location, whether out in the garden or a container, so that the herbs have access to maximum conditions that support their growth.

Tip #3: Buy seeds from reputable companies to ensure that you are handling herbs whose genetic makeup is intact.

Tip #4: To preserve the nutritional content of your herbs, you can do drying and freeze, among other methods of preservation.

Frequently Asked Questions about Herb Gardening

Which herbs can I begin with?

The truth is, hundreds of herbs are available in repositories, and you can cultivate for their medicinal and culinary benefits. However, the most important factors that you have to consider when choosing the right herbs will be what you want to grow, and other essential conditions that support your herbs of choice such as the soil and the climate.

The best thing is for you to assess a list of herbs that you have in mind and determine which ones you are your favorite and fit into the growth conditions available in your location.

What cultural requirements do the herbs have?

For each herb to thrive well, you must know the required conditions for their optimal growth. Other plants also can self-propagate, in which case you are fortunate if one of your herbs does this. Self-propagation refers to the ability of a plant to self-reproduce either by reseeding, layering, cutting, among other ways.

The most important thing is to pay close attention to the amount of sun the herbs need each day. The information that you can get from journals, and if it says that they need it for 4-6 hours in a day, then it probably needs just that! The other thing is water requirements and the soil type it needs. It ensures that they get optimal conditions for optimal growth and development.

Which herbs can I start within my weather?

When it comes to the choice of herbs to plant in your climate, you can replicate each herb's requirements. For instance, most of the herbs do well with less water, 4-6 hours of sunlight exposure and average quality soil.

However, when it comes to winter temperatures, the conditions cannot be compromised. It means that you have to be within the zone that your herbs of choice can thrive. You can also find this information available at the nursery where these herb seedlings are raised.

The truth is, determining the kinds of herbs that will do well within your area. You will realize that is you come from a place where the conditions are delicate; you can grow a few of those that need this kind of terms specifically. You can also substitute those you cannot grow in your area.

Should I raise my herbs from seeds?

Seeds are the best when it comes to herb gardening, especially if you are a beginner. Remember that we have mentioned getting seeds from reputable companies that have not genetically engineered their components. In fact, rather than getting your seeds just from one company, you can get them from at least two companies.

It is also crucial that you ensure that you have read the herb's descriptions well.

The best thing is to consider a suitable vendor to work. To do that, consider asking yourself the following questions;

Which company meets the criteria you are looking?

Will the company be a suitable resource for educational materials?

If their process of ordering helpful?

What is their client service?

Do they have ethical considerations when it comes to GMOs, hybrid seeds and SEMINIS?

Don't worry if you feel like you are not ready yet to raise herbs from seeds. The truth is that you will finally get where you are going, and the best thing is for you to start with the goal in mind.

Where can I find herb plants?

If you desire to start a medicinal or culinary herb garden, there is a good chance that you will exhaust so many resources available in local nurseries within a couple of years. It is because, by the time you have mastered all that information, you will already be herb-savvy! It is because you will have moved from pure herbs like basil to a broader and more intricate variety.

However, if you are specifically looking for culinary and medicinal herbs, the best place you can get them is from Horizon Herbs. The best thing with this place is that they offer you satisfactory answers to your questions that revolve around; what seeds are viable. They also have packets, catalogs, and experts who are knowledgeable about herbs. They sell container herbs and cuttings from the roots, which can be very helpful, especially if you do not wish to start from growing seeds.

Can I grow herbs from seeds?

If you have a friend, family or local nursery growing herbs, you can gather information from them on the best methods of rooting or cutting for that particular herb and then try to replicate the same.

For instance, what I have found out about thyme over the years is that they can be propagated so well and easily by layering. It is how you can achieve successful layering by first taking a supple thyme stem that is mature and sits it in the soil.

Use a garden pin to weight that down. Ensure that you have it watered well and then wait for it to begin sprouting at the soil surface. Then cut it off to get new herbs. Hence no seed required.

Again, you must ensure that you have reference material on hand. It is also vital for you to learn how to perform wild crafts, especially for those plants that you have available and where it is legal.

Amount of space needed

Here, the best answer is for you to determine what space you have available for herb gardening. If you live in an urban apartment, you must consider what to grow in your deck, window or patio facing the southern direction.

On the other hand, you may have a friend that has a farm backyard or an extra space in their yard that they can give you to grow your herbs. After all, it is said, if you are into herb gardening, you have to get in touch with your creative self. The bottom line is for you to look for sufficient space to cultivate your herbs.

When determining the amount of space you need for your herbs; you have to ask yourself:

Are there people growing this herb?

How many plants will take the available space?

How much space is enough for the herbs you intend to plant? If their lots of shade, unusable ground or is the entire space available?

What you have to note is that you need to know your herbs well and work with your plan. The truth is that it does not matter how much time it takes for the grasses to mature. What truly matters is being able to use that time well to learn more about herbal preparations, their uses, and properties. You have to be willing to know your herbs themselves as they grow and when they occasionally fail.

My advice is that you should take your time and pace yourself. But what is even relevant is for you to start this year and start planning and planting your herbal garden. It does not matter how small the effort is; the key is for you to grow what you will use and what will grow. The sooner you embrace container gardening, the better for you will be at this.

General Upkeep

Apart from watering and fertilizing, what else does the vegetable container garden need? Consider the following tasks:

•Staking and framework - You may have chosen plants that require some support or other form of climbing apparatus. Be sure that you install these things at the time you plant seeds or transplants. Be sure that you are using safe plant materials to tie these plants to their growing structures, and to continually gauge them for their ratio of above the soil growth/weight to below the soil counterweights.

•Deadheading - A lot of container gardeners forget that some of their plants will need pruning and deadheading if they are to produce the number of blooms or produce indicated. Take the time to discover what the best methods might be. For instance, you will want to know how to pinch or prune tomatoes to keep them at the level of control you require. The same can be said for many plants and flowers, so do a bit of research to discover what is best for your plants.

•Monitor for pests - There is little that you can do to prevent pests from finding your plants, so be as vigilant about them with your container gardens as possible. Because the world of a single container is so small, a single invasion of caterpillars or insects can decimate the miniature garden in a matter of days or even hours. Be aware of signs of disease, too, as this can mean that a contagious problem is at hand. Quarantine any containers that seem to be affected and take all possible action as soon as you notice any issues.

•Consider reflections - Many container gardeners forget that heat and light can be a bit overwhelming to potted plants. For example, a container garden on a patio paved with white stones or concrete is getting sunlight from almost every angle. It is because the light is reflecting upon the plants as well as shining from above. Try to keep this sort of double threat in mind and provide plants with shade, if possible.

•Have emergency plans - Do you live in an area prone to violent thunderstorms, hail, or other extremes? If so, try to consider what this might mean to the container garden. If you can offer some sort of protection when severe weather, or even early frosts, are forecast, it can save a lot of heartbreak and waste.

•Replacements - If you took our advice about making succession plantings to keep yourself supplied with things all season, be sure that you are preparing the soil for each new crop. Try not to double up on the same item on the same ground over and over again during the summer. Make some plans to have replacements ready, but to make them different than the plants before them. It helps to keep the soil in your containers as healthy and rich as possible and also cut back on the risks of disease.

You will get into a good rhythm with the container garden. You will find that it becomes a charming habit to head to the various pots and containers to see what might be ready to eat, how individual plants are doing, and just to enjoy the sights, smells, and textures of growing things.

Unfortunately, like most good things, your garden will have to reach its end as the season's change. The growing season may last 3/4 of the year where you are, or it could be less than 1/3 of the year. No matter what, you will have a lot of end of season tasks to consider.

These will include:

•Removing frost killed or depleted plants from the containers - start a wonderful compost heap by tossing all of the dead or expired plants into the mix, and also consider using the potting soil in a pile as well.

•Empty pots and scrub them clean with a bleach mixture (10% works best) to ensure that no fungal issues remain.

•Put fragile or vulnerable pots into storage.

•Prepare overwintering plants by surrounding heavy or immovable planters that contain perennials and woody plants with straw and wrapping with burlap. (Note: You can avoid the need to do this by using smaller containers inside oversized containers and simply lifting the potted plants out for overwintering in more controlled conditions such as a root cellar or insulated garden shed)

•Dig a protective trench for smaller plants in containers and place them in the channel, covered with soil and straw for the winter months. Water them in well until the first frosts arrive. (Note: This will not work with clay pots. Simply remove their plants and lay the plants in the trench with the other potted plants, and store the clay vessels indoors)

Once the garden has been prepared for colder weather, you can start to make plans for the upcoming season. Many container gardeners spend happy hours during the winter months looking through seed and plant catalogs and developing strategies to expand their garden during the following season.

Conclusion: Vegetable Gardening in Containers

Thank you for making it to the end. While fertilizing, watering and weeding are the big three, there are still a few maintenance tasks which you are going to need to do if you want to keep your garden healthy. There are also a couple tasks that you'll have to do if you want to make sure that your harvest goes smoothly and the veggies themselves are high quality. None of these tasks will take you very long, and a few of them only need to be done once, maybe twice, per crop. But skipping out on these tasks is a bad idea as doing so needlessly puts your garden at risk.

Some of these tasks could arguably be considered pest control and disease prevention techniques, such as removing dead plant matter which could harbor both. They are important enough to merit a discussion here as well. You should be building your pest control behaviors into your general garden maintenance routine so that you are never caught unprepared by an unexpected infestation or infection.

Always remember to disinfect your tools after use. This is a common sense maintenance task that you wouldn't believe how many gardeners ignore. The reason it is ignored is likely one of ignorance and a lack of knowledge. Plants are living creatures. They not only have a living biology but they can communicate their needs to us in their visual language. You should disinfect all of your tools, including your shovels, rakes or hoes. Still, you especially need to disinfect shears or anything else that has come into contact with the plants themselves. Trimming a plant is essentially a form of surgery. Imagine going in for an operation and finding out the surgeon used a dirty scalpel to cut you open. You wouldn't be surprised at all when the wound got infected or you caught a new disease. Yet many gardeners leave their tools dirty and use them again and again, only to be surprised when their plants end up sick. Always disinfect your tools at the end of the day after using them.

Remove Dead Plant Matter. Another step that is often forgotten about is the removal of dead plant matter. A lot of beginner gardeners don't see a problem with a dead plant matter in their beds, but leaving dead plant matter in and around your garden is one of the worst things you can do if you want your plants to stay healthy. The problem isn't the dead matter itself. The plant matter is dead; it's not going to do any harm. The problem is in what this matter attracts. Dead plant matter is a breeding ground for pests and disease. Pests can hide in this plant waste, feeding off it while it is still fresh and then moving on to your plants shortly afterwards. It is a good idea to check your garden daily to clear out your dead. If this is too much work for you then at least clean out the beds whenever you go to water them, as long as you don't let any dead and rotting plant matter stick around for too long, you will most likely be okay.

COMPANION PLANTING:

THE ULTIMATE BEGINNER'S GUIDE TO COMPANION GARDENING; A CHEMICAL FREE METHOD TO GROW ORGANIC AND HEALTHY VEGETABLES AT HOME DETERRING PESTS AND INCREASING YIELD.

BY EDWARD GREEN

COMPANION

PLANTING

THE ULTIMATE BEGINNERS GUIDE TO COMPANION
GARDENING. A CHEMICAL FREE METHOD TO
GROW ORGANIC AND HEALTHY VEGETABLES AT HOME
DETERRING PESTS AND INCREASING YIELD

EDWARD GREEN

Introduction: Companion Planting

A successful garden is based on maximizing use of space, increasing crop productivity, pollination and pest control. Companion planting, meaning planting different crops in proximity, is beneficial for all of these things and more.

In the past few years, companion planting is receiving a lot of attention from the scientific community because it can help reduce the need for harmful chemicals in farming. Home gardeners are re-discovering this information and using it to their benefit.

This book is made to teach you how to start Companion Planting and grow a successful garden full of healthy vegetables, fruits and herbs that all benefit from each other to grow better.

In order to start, keep in consideration the following:

Seasonality is a basic rule of thumb when considering companion planting: for example, radishes and greens grow well together, as they both like cold temperatures and well-drained soil; tomatoes and squash grow well together, as they both like lots of suns and do well in the heat, while peppers also thrive at this time of year and provide some natural pest repellent.

Space can also be a common-sense product of companion planting wisdom: planting lower growing herbs such as tarragon, oregano, and rosemary in between tomato plants give vines room to spread while also providing pest protection. Also, sequential planting is another sub-category of companion planting—planting continuously throughout the year—has the added benefit of discouraging weed growth.

These are merely a handful of examples of the vast reserve of material concerning the benefits and techniques of companion planting. Farmers Almanacs, farmers' markets, cooperative extension services are all excellent places to get further advice on how to set up your garden for maximum success.

What is Companion Gardening?

What is Companion Gardening and the Science behind It

Companion gardening is simply a form of Polyculture. When used intelligently along with gardening techniques such as Raised Bed Gardening or Container Gardening, for instance, then it is the method of sharing the mutual benefits of the individual plants, is capable of producing fantastic results. Companion planting is likened to putting together the perfect partnership, creating results in respect of more abundant, healthier crops that the individual plants could not produce.

The fact is that, just like we homo-sapiens, plants need good companions to thrive and flourish in their environment. Unlike us, however, is rooted to the spot, they cannot choose their friends – we have to choose friends or companions for them! We take into account the strong points and needs of the individual plants and then put them together – in fact, the gardener takes on the role of match-maker!

Will I bet you never considered running a dating agency for vegetables before this – did you? Joking apart; the fact is that if the plants thrive – alongside the ideal companions that you have provided - then the harvest is bountiful – and everyone is happy.

Companion planting is nothing new; and is reasonably well documented. The Chinese, for instance, have been using this method to protect and promote their rice crops for over 1,000 years.

By planting the mosquito fern as a companion for their rice crops, that hosts a special CYANOBACTERIUM that fixes nitrogen from the atmosphere. It also helps to block out the light so that competing weeds cannot prosper, the rice being planted when it is tall enough to stick above the fern.

The native Indians of North America are widely accredited for pioneering the 'Three Sisters' technique of planting corn, beans and squash together. The corn would act as a trellis for the beans, which in turn laid down nitrogen that benefited the corn and the squash. Sunflowers could also be grown, usually a short distance away from the three sisters to act help draw away aphids.

Companion planting, although ancient in origin, has grown up alongside the whole Organic Farming movement. With the emphasis on healthier foods, organically grown, this holistic approach to growing vegetables has taken on whole new importance for the modern, environmentally aware grower.

What are the Benefits of Companion Gardening

Many reasons can be cited to promote the idea of companion planting, from environmental to personal. Here are just five of the most important reasons:

1. Environmental

Protecting the environment is a hugely important issue these days and rightly so. If more people got themselves involved with the principles behind organic and companion gardening, then we would not be polluting both our bodies and the land, with chemical fertilizers or poisonous insecticides to the extent that we are.

It does not just involve ourselves but has ramifications for generations to come.

Millions of tons of waste going into landfills every year, which in fact could easily be recycled – to our benefit! Composting is a part of growing your vegetables, and becoming more environmentally aware is one way to help balance its wastage.

It can be correctly stated that companion planting, when done in concert with other organic growing methods, is good for our bodies and good for the environment – a win-win situation.

2. Productivity

The main principle behind companion planting is the fact that when individual plants are grown together, then they benefit from one another or at least the different plants can be grown together because they have different needs. It means that they are not competing for the same nutrients or even atmospheric conditions.

With It being the case, then it also means that you can have a higher volume of plants in the same growing area, as they can be grown closer together without it being detrimental in any way –, if done correctly, they will benefit from It closeness.

3. Easy maintenance:

The reason that companion planting generally means easier maintenance is that it may not at first be recognized. However, the fact is that if the plants are appropriately chosen, it means that they are planted closer together, meaning less of an area to cover when maintaining or harvesting your vegetables.

It is especially relevant in a raised bed situation, where the area you have to cover is limited to the confines of the raised bed.

In It situation you have a 'double score' so to speak; as a raised bed garden is not so prone to weeds anyway, It coupled with correct companion planting, where the sunshine and nutrients are denied to weeds; leads to a situation where you can maximize your efforts and get better results.

4. Natural insect control:

One of the big pluses for the companion planter is the fact that fewer insect problems occur if the plants accompanying their neighbors are correctly chosen. For instance, if onions or leeks are planted alongside carrots, then problems with the dreaded carrot fly are less of an issue as the smell of the onions detracts the fly from the carrots.

Marigolds planted alongside your tomatoes will attract hoverflies, which will protect them against aphids.

More examples to follow!

5. Less need for fertilizer

Again, if done correctly using organic methods of growing your vegetables, then there will be little if any need for fertilizer.

The reason is two-fold. Firstly good organic compost in your growing area means that fertilizer should not be needed unless you are perhaps aiming to grow 'super crops.'

Secondly, if the plants are appropriately rotated, then the needs of one plant may be supplied by the waste or productivity of another. For instance, legumes like peas and beans can draw nitrogen from the atmosphere and deposit it into the ground. It benefits a multitude of other plants that flourish in nitrogen-rich soil.

Companion Gardening Methods

Companion gardening has been practiced in many different ways that vary from place to place. While many people know the term companion gardening, there are obscure lines that have in the recent past arisen between the practice and other forms of smart gardening. In short, it may be possible that so many people are practicing organic gardening, only that they refer to it with a different word and are oblivious of the fact that they are doing it. Below are the significant methods of companion gardening.

1. Square foot Gardening

Square foot gardening is a practice that attempts to protect plants from traditional gardening woes by planting them on particular soil as well as close to each other. Crops are planted on hybrid soil, which is a mixture of compost, peat and vermiculite. The soil has all the nutrients that re needed for the crops to thrive. After this, the soil is placed in an isolated environment where it does not mix with other soils and crops planted on each square foot of the garden. To create a picture of what the ideal farm must be, the gardener divides the top of the box with strips that mark out boxes that are equal in size. In each square foot, the farmer will plant a different crop, thus effectively growing more than ten types of crops in a single sixteen square meter space.

It method generally achieves better results than traditional companion cropping as the crops are grown close together, and they are thus able to interact and form a rigid front against pests and deceases.

2. Forest Garden

Forest gardening refers to creating a plant ecosystem from scratch. It is done by planting a forest and increasingly planting smaller crops between the rows. They planted crops also form a shade or host to an additional row, which leads to a very vast ecosystem. Its system has up to seven levels of growth, and plants can be planted of up to 14 varieties, alternating between plants of different varieties in the rows. Plants are grown in woodlands where they cover each other and help each other grow and also resist pests and deceases. In elephant infested woodlands, for instance, crops may be protected by simply adding an extra row of pepper in the garden. It will keep the jumbos off the farm. It may also help keep primates off the gardens too. Forest gardening opens up a new way of intercropping or simply companion cropping as the crops will help each other in different stages of growth.

3. Organic Gardening

It is the most common type of companion gardening. Organic gardening generally refers to a type of gardening where the farmer will avoid the use of inorganic materials and inputs in growing the garden. The basic idea of this is that the farmer will use companion crops to fight off each other's pests as well as discourage disease spread. Organic gardening emphasizes natural farm inputs as opposed to extreme use of chemicals, which is encouraging companion crops to be substituted for chemicals. It also encourages farmers to have some real natural barriers to pests and disease, some of which are other crops. In the end, there is a myriad of names that draw their concept from companion gardening and will thus be most likely to be called by their other names. However, the idea behind all this is almost always companion gardening. Thus, organic gardening is simply a fancy and advanced form of companion gardening.

4. Spatial Interaction

Spatial interactions involve placing individual plants that affect other plants in the same vicinity. These interactions can be chemical, benefiting the growth of the other plant, or they could attract beneficial insects to your garden.

5. Nurse Cropping

Methods of nurse cropping include the Seven Layer System, where some larger plants shield the smaller ones.

6. Three Sisters Method

It is the method with the planting of three different veggies together with each plant benefitting the others. Corn, beans and squash are the typical combinations used in the Three Sisters Method, but there are others as well.

7. Container Gardens

Container gardens consist of simple plastic five-gallon buckets with or without an automated watering system built-in. These container gardens minimize weeds; help you eliminate problems with poor soil with the added benefit of being able to rearrange individual plants after they begin growing.

8. Layer System

The seven-layer system utilizes the size and type of plants in what is called a 'forest garden.' These plants and trees grow together, with each benefiting the others.

- The Canopy Layer: is made up of large fruit or nut trees (not walnut trees). These trees provide the shade or canopy that protects the sixth layer plants (the ground cover) from too much sun exposure and excess winds. These trees also provide support for the seventh layer of plants, which are the climbers or vine plants.

- Low Tree Layer: includes the dwarf fruit trees that sit under the canopy of the more giant trees.
- Shrub Layer: consists of the bushes that grow berries and other types of fruits. These are protected by both the more giant trees and the low tree layer.
- Herbaceous Layer: are the beets or herbs that grow in the shade of the hedge.
- RHIZOSPHERE Layer: Root vegetables like carrots, potatoes and more are the RHIZOSPHERE Layer. They benefit from the shade and the water that the more giant trees bring up from the water table.
- Soil Surface: These are the ground cover in the first layer. These include strawberries. The ground cover prevents weeds from infiltrating the ecosystem and provides yet another beneficial fruit in your garden.
- Vertical Layer: Also, in the first layer, the Vertical Layer includes cucumbers, grapes and other vine fruits and vegetables.

Allelopathy

ALLELOPATHY is best described as chemical warfare between plants. One plant can suppress another and to take advantage of that situation. The word is derived from two Ancient Greek words, 'ALLELON,' meaning each other and 'pathos' which means to suffer.

Therefore, ALLELOPATHIC plants deliberately create adverse growing conditions that stunt and kill off neighboring plants. It can be by reducing germination rates or seedling growth or just plain killing off competing plants. Used wisely, ALLELOPATHIC plants can be a great alternative to chemicals!

Plants compete for resources such as space, water, nutrition, and sunlight. Some compete by snowballing; others spread out wide or send down deep roots. Other plants have developed analytic tools for getting the resources they require to flourish.

ALLELOPATHIC plants release compounds from the roots into the soil, which then suppress or kill their neighbors as they are sucked up through their root systems. These harmful chemicals are unsurprising, known as ALLELOCHEMICALS. Some of these chemicals can go as far as changing the level of chlorophyll production, which can then slow down or even stop photosynthesis, which leads to the death of the plant.

A lot of ALLELOPATHIC plants release chemicals in gas form from small pores in their leaves. As their neighbors absorb these gasses, they are either suppressed or killed.

Some ALLELOPATHIC plants deal with the competition when their leaves fall to the ground. The leaves decompose and release chemicals that then inhibit nearby plants.

There are a lot of different plants that have ALLELOPATHIC tendencies, but it isn't particularly common. Sometimes, however, you can very quickly plant an ALLELOPATHIC plant near one of its victims without realizing it and wonder why some of your plants struggle to grow.

The black walnut tree is probably the master of chemical warfare in the plant kingdom. Its leaves, roots, nut hulls and buds have ALLELOPATHIC properties, and it also secretes JUGLONE into the soil, which inhibits respiration in many plants. The black walnut guards its resources so jealously that virtually nothing will grow near to one. Many a gardener has rejoiced at the black walnut tree in their garden until they realized that nothing would grow near it.

ALLELOPATHIC characteristics can be found in any part of a plant, whether it is the root, bark, flowers, seeds, fruits, leaves, or pollen. It varies from plant to plant, though the majority of plants store their ALLELOPATHIC chemicals in their leaves.

Some common plants that are known to have ALLELOPATHIC properties include:

• English laurel

• Elderberry

• Bearberry

• Rhododendron

• Junipers, which hamper the growth of grasses

• Perennial rye hampers the growth of apple trees

• Sugar maple hampers the growth of yellow birch and white spruce

If you think about where you see these plants growing, you will see very little growing underneath or near them.

There is a lot of research underway into ALLELOPATHIC plants, and the list of plants is regularly being updated. These plants are exciting to farmers for their properties, which could well find their way into genetically modified seeds.

The advantage of ALLELOCHEMICALS is that they can produce natural herbicides and pesticides. Planting the right plants together as companions will keep down certain weeds, which can reduce reliance on chemical herbicides. When pairings are chosen well, the ALLELOPATHIC plant will even have a positive effect on your chosen vegetable crop.

ALLELOPATHIC research is still very much in its infancy as researchers try to understand its interaction between plants. Some research papers published, and you can use this effect to your benefit in your garden. If you have established plants already present in your garden and are struggling to grow anything else, it may be that one of these plants has ALLELOPATHIC properties.

Be aware that ALLELOCHEMICALS can build up in the soil, and it can take several years for the levels of these chemicals to drop so that other plants will grow. Years ago, I removed an English laurel tree from my garden as it was too large. Underneath was bare soil. Nothing had grown there, but when I dug over the soil and added manure, everything I planted died. It was several years and a lot of fertilizer and compost before anything would grow in that area again. If you have to remove ALLELOPATHIC plants, then you may want to consider removing 12-18 inches of soil and replacing it if you struggle to get anything to grow in that space.

Insects: The Good Ones and the Bad Ones

Beneficial Insects for Your Garden

The good news is that insect pests are far outnumbered by insect allies in our gardens and yards. Without bees, no flower will be pollinated, and in this regard, many kinds of moths and flies make their contribution. Many beneficial insects prey on pest insects, and parasitic insects will lay their eggs right inside the pest insects. When the larvae hatch, they usually kill or at least weaken their hosts. Other ally insects like flies and dung beetles assist in the breaking down of decaying matter in the garden and so help to build good fertile soil. Therefore, I will name the fourteen most beneficial insects to have around and how you can lure them to your garden and convince them to make it their new home.

- **Wasps and Bees**

Bees

There is a good reason why people in agricultural circles refer to honeybees as their 'spark plugs.' They are essential for pollinating crops. However; they are not the only pollinators around; wild bees make their contribution as well and act as agents of pest control on top of it all. Pollen and nectar are used by all bees to feed on; they also gather it for their nests. It is the main distinction between them and hornets and wasps.

They fly from one flower to another in their quest for food and, in the process, distribute pollen grains amongst the different flowers they visit, pollinating blooms as they go along.

It has not yet been determined what the cause of its disorder is, but what we know is that the worker bees just suddenly start to die, leaving their queen bee, nursing bees and as yet unborn brood without the necessary support. Eventually, the whole hive collapses. Speculation is rife; maybe it is caused by parasites or diseases, maybe the damage done by chemical pesticides to their nervous and immune systems.

Luckily our tiny little 'sweet bees,' bumblebees and other natives are still active and doing their bit to pollinate garden plants and crops. So, how can you encourage these native bees? Plant enough flowers to last the bees as long as possible. Allow some bare, open ground for them where they can tunnel and build their nests. Also, make sure they have access to water in a shallow container.

Yellow Jackets

Hornets and yellow jackets are feared by most people, but they have an essential role to play as pest predators. Diving into foliage, they target caterpillars, flies and larvae, which they feed to their offspring. So, unless someone in your family is allergic to their stings or they are living in an area frequented by pets and people, do not destroy their nests.

Beetles

Ground Beetles

Ground beetles are blue-black, swift-footed, and hideaway under boards and stone during the daylight hours. Come to the darkness of night, and they emerge to feed on slug and snail eggs, cutworms and root maggots. They even climb trees in search of tent caterpillars and armyworms. Large populations can live in gardens underneath the stone pathways, semi-permanent mulched vegetable or flower beds or the undisturbed groundcovers of orchards.

Lady Beetles

Everyone knows lady beetles with their hard, shiny bodies. There are around three thousand species in total, and they prey on soft, small pests like spider mites, MEARLYBUGS and aphids. I have to mention that not all the species are right for your garden, for example, the Mexican bean beetle. The larvae, as well as the adult beetles, will feed on pests. The larvae resemble tiny miniature alligators with their tapered bodies and branching spines. You can buy convergent ladybugs at some garden centers. They overwinter in mass where they are collected. But it is not easy to keep them in your garden unless you have a greenhouse.

Rove Beetles

Rove beetles have elongated bodies with stubby, short wings, resembling earwigs' pinchers. They are active decomposers and will work away at plant material and manure. Others prey on root maggots.

Flies

The TACHINID Fly

These flies are dark gray, bristly and large and lay their larvae or eggs on stinkbugs, corn borers, caterpillars and cutworms amongst other pests. They are quite effective against the outbreaks of armyworm and tent caterpillar.

The SYRPHID Fly

These flies are also called hover or flower flies. They are easily recognizable by their black and white or yellow stripes. Still, They are also often mistakenly identified as yellow jackets or even bees. After laying their eggs inside aphids, their larvae devour the aphids. The larvae are translucent, unattractive gray maggots and resemble small slugs, so do not be misled by their appearance.

Aphid Midges

The larva of this fly is a tiny orange maggot and will feed voraciously on aphids. They can be purchased at commercial insectaries. Release them into your greenhouse, and you will see the positive effects very soon.

Insects That Don't Benefit the Garden and How to Get Rid of Them Naturally

Bad Insects

While the perfect garden would only attract beneficial insects that would prey on anything and everything that dared step foot into the garden, that's rarely the case. Most gardens contain a wide variety of insects, both good and bad.

Let's take a closer look at some of the more common pests found in gardens across the country. If you're lucky, you won't have to deal with more than one or two of these insects at once.

Aphids

Aphids, also known as plant lice, can have up to 12 live babies per day. Within the first week, one aphid can have 84 babies. Within a week, those aphids are ready to start having babies of their own. The 84 babies will start adding 12 babies apiece per day, which is more than 1,000 aphids being added daily. Once they start having babies, the numbers jump even more dramatically. Within a month, millions of aphids will be infesting the garden. Of course, this simple scenario assumes no aphids die and that each of the aphids has exactly 12 babies per day, but you get the point.

Luckily, you have some options when it comes to control aphids. You can plant caraway, chamomile, dandelions, buckwheat and tansy to attract insects that prey on them. Ladybugs, green lacewings, praying mantises, and minute pirate bugs will all make a meal of aphids. Nasturtiums can be used as a trap crop for aphids.

Additionally, you can use the following plants to repel aphids

- Basil.

- Catnip.

- Chives.

- Clover.

- Coriander.

- Dill.

- Eucalyptus.

- Fennel.

- Garlic.

- Onions.

- Nettles.

- Peppermint.

- Radishes.

Caterpillars

To keep caterpillars at bay, add plants to your garden that draw in parasitic wasps, praying mantises and green lacewings. Another option is to hang a bird feeder to call in birds that'll come for the bird food and supplement their meals with any caterpillars that cross their paths. When you see a caterpillar, handpick it and move it far from your garden.

The following plants can be planted in a garden to repel caterpillars:

• Lavender.

• Peppermint.

• Sage.

Colorado potato beetle

The Colorado potato beetle looks like a yellowish-orange ladybug with stripes instead of dots. While ladybugs are a preferred predator in the garden and will eat Colorado potato beetles, these pests will quickly defoliate peppers, potatoes, eggplant and tomatoes. In addition to ladybugs, nematodes are beneficial to have around when potato beetles are present.

Some sources indicate the Colorado potato beetle doesn't like to walk over coarse mulch. Adding a layer of straw mulch around your plants may prevent the beetle from making it to your plants.

The following plants will repel Colorado potato beetles:

- Catnip.

- Chives.

- Coriander.

- Eucalyptus.

- Garlic.

- Green beans.

- Marigolds.

- Nasturtiums.

- Peas.

Flea Beetles

These tiny little pests are found across the entirety of North America. They chew small, round holes in the leaves of most vegetables and will jump around nervously when disturbed. Flea beetles prefer dry soil to lay their eggs in, so keep your soil damp to make your garden less attractive. Nematodes can be added to the soil to make short work of any larvae that do hatch.

The following plants will repel flea beetles:

• Catnip.

• Peppermint.

• Rue.

• Thyme.

Mexican bean beetle

The Mexican bean beetle is a connoisseur of several varieties of beans. It has a bottomless pit for a stomach and will continue chewing on the leaves of a plant until it starts to die. These beetles roam the Western half of the United States, looking for bean crops to devastate.

The following plants are known to repel Mexican bean beetles

• Garlic.

• Marigolds.

• Rosemary.

Japanese Beetles

Japanese beetles are commonly found in the Eastern half of the United States. They are known to attack a variety of vegetables and flowers. They're a bluish-green color and feature rust-colored wing covers. They're pretty to look at, but the damage they can do to a crop is anything but pretty.

The following plants will deter Japanese beetles:

• Catnip.

- Chives.

- Chrysanthemums.

- Garlic.

- Marigolds.

- Onions.

- Rue.

Scales

Scales are aptly named because, at a glance, they look like small scales attached to a plant. They're destructive little creatures that will suck sap from plants during every stage of their life cycle. When you notice scales on your plants, prune them back to get rid of the affected areas or scrub them off the branches.

There are no plants that are known to deter scales, so you'll have to rely on predatory insects to get the job done. Ladybugs, praying mantises, and green lacewings will all dine on scales, so plants that attract them may help.

Tomato FRUITWORMS (Corn Earworms)

Tomato FRUITWORMS, also known as corn earworms, cotton bollworms and geranium budworms, are found in gardens throughout North America. These worms are known by several names, usually indicative of the type of plant they're attacking. They've been known to dine on cotton, beans, peas, peppers, tomatoes, corn, geraniums, potatoes and squash.

The adults are small moths that lay eggs on the bottoms of leaves. The larvae feed on the leaves as they grow. If they're attacking a corn crop, they'll move into the husks as the corn matures and will eventually begin to feed on the silk and the corn kernels at the ends of the ears.

Geraniums and thyme are known to deter the tomato FRUITWORMS.

Tomato Hornworm

This giant caterpillar is found in gardens throughout the United States, usually munching on the leaves of eggplant, peppers, potatoes and tomatoes. They develop into giant moths that have a wingspan of up to 5".

The following plants will repel tomato hornworms:

- Borage

- Dill

- Thyme

Full Sun or Partial Shade Garden (Lighting)

One of the most significant decisions you're going to have to make is whether you're going to grow a full sun or a partial shade garden. If you're limited on space, It decision may have already been made for you, and you're going to have to work with what you've got. The amount of sun and shade an area gets is one of the major determining factors of the types of plants that can be grown there.

Most fruits and vegetables prefer full sun, so if you're looking to grow a produce garden, that's the way to go.

That isn't to say they all prefer sitting in the middle of a desert baking in hot sunlight. Full sun is defined as at least 6 hours of sunlight per day, while some plants need as many as 8 to 10 hours per day to thrive. Trying to grow plants that require full sun in an area that gets less exposure to the sun than this will be an exercise in frustration. The plants may grow, but yields will be reduced, and they'll be more susceptible to attack from pests and disease.

Partial shade or partial sun implies a plant needs less sunlight and can get by on 3 to 6 hours of sunlight per day. These plants do best when they're shaded from the sun in the afternoon when it's at its peak. Placing a plant that prefers partial shade or partial sun in an area that gets full sunlight can scorch the plant when temperatures start to climb, causing it to wilt or even die.

Full shade means relatively little sunlight. There may be a small handful of plants you can grow in full shade, but without much light, you're going to be very limited. If you want to plant fruit and vegetables, you're going to have to find another spot.

Most vegetables, fruits and herbs prefer full sunlight. If you have a garden that only gets partial sunlight, you're going to have to select plants that can be grown with only partial sunlight. There isn't a whole lot you can do to increase the amount of sunlight an area gets short of chopping down trees, moving mountains or tearing down buildings. Reflective mulches can be used to reflect sunlight up to plants, but the effect is minimal.

Lettuce, spinach, radishes and some varieties of strawberries are well-suited to partially-shaded garden areas. Other crops like peas and potatoes will grow in partial shade, but yields will be reduced. To be clear, these plants will still need sunlight to grow—they just don't need as much as some of the needier plants.

Those looking to grow plants that require partial shade in a full sun location have a handful of options at their disposal. For one, you can build a structure that provides shade during certain times of the day. It's best to build a shade that provides relief from the afternoon sun, as opposed to one that provides shade in the morning. Afternoon sunlight is hotter and more likely to damage plants than morning sunlight. Another option is to set up latticework through which the sun can shine. Your plants will get sunlight throughout the day, but won't be exposed to the constant heat of the sun. Some plants will do better than others with It technique, so experiment to find out what works best.

You may be wondering what all this has to do with companion planting. Some plants grow tall or have large leaves that spread out that can be used to provide shade to smaller plants. The larger plants can be planted as companion plants to smaller plants that need partial shade. Corn, sunflowers, tomatoes and artichokes can all be planted to provide shade for smaller plants. Trellises plants like pole beans and grapes are also an excellent way to provide dappled sunlight, which is the light that's filtered through the leaves of the trellised plant.

These larger sun-loving plants can be planted to provide shade for plants like cabbage, broccoli and cauliflower that don't do well when temperatures start to climb as summer approaches. Smaller plants like carrots, cucumbers and lettuce can also benefit from being planted in the shade of a taller plant as long as the taller plants don't surround them and completely block out the sun.

Trees can be used to provide shade, but you have to be careful not to use a variety of tree that's going to grow to great heights and completely block sunlight from reaching your garden. If trees are already present and are providing too much shade, you may be able to top them or prune them back to ensure your garden gets ample sunlight.

Planning Your Garden

Before you start your companion garden, like any project that you intend to build successfully, you will need to draw up some plans. The plan for this type of garden may contain the following seven significant steps:

Make a List of the Vegetables You Need To Grow

Everything starts with a list. You must have a list of all the vegetables you will need for your family. Depending upon what type of garden you want to grow, you will have to determine the best options for the region in which you are residing. Each region has its seasonal vegetables, fruits, and herbs. You will need to plan so you can make the most of what you can grow naturally with the least amount of effort. In case you are looking for vegetables that do not typically grow in your region, you can always consider building a small greenhouse.

Identify the Best Companion Plants for Your Vegetables

Once you decide what vegetables you want to grow, the logical step is to find out what are the best companion plants for your garden. Do refer to Table No one shown earlier regarding the best matches between plants. While the list is not all-inclusive, it does give a good idea about how to go about pairing your favorite vegetable plants to ensure that you have an outstanding harvest.

To help you decide what companion plants to choose, take into account what type of beneficial pests, beneficial insects/ animals/ and micro-organisms your vegetables will usually attract in the region in which you live, then chose those plants that will help your garden the most. Seek the assistance of an expert in the first 1-2 years if you are not sure what to do. After some time, you will gain enough experience to make your own decisions.

Draw a Map of the Garden

Draw a map of your garden and annotate where you want your plants to be planted. It is imperative to have this map because you will have to rotate the places of the vegetables every year to ensure that the soil will remain fertile and rich enough to encourage the optimal growth of your favorite vegetables. For the best results, you would need to rotate the placement every year or at the most once every two years.

While drawing up the map of the garden, you should keep in mind that the taller plants should be positioned such that they should not overshadow the smaller plants. For a garden to grow well, each plant should have adequate (as per the need of the plant) access to sunshine, shade, and water.

Calculate the Sowing Date

Each plant has a particular sowing date. You will need to calculate the right time to plant the vegetables so you will not lose your harvest owing to unfavorable climatic conditions. To know the sowing date, you will need to subtract the growth period from the planting date. It is the date when you should sow seeds indoors, outdoors, or in a greenhouse to have the seedlings ready for transplant after the last frost. Table No two will help gather an idea about this exercise.

Here it is important to note that you should know which vegetable will grow well if seeds are sown directly in the garden soil and which seeds need to be "started" indoors or in a greenhouse for transplanting once the frost is gone. The last date of frost in your climatic region can be readily ascertained from an almanac

Calculating Sowing Date

Seed/Plant	Write in Sow Date	Growth Period # of Weeks	Safe Set-Out Date (Relative to Last Frost)
Beans*		8 to 10	
Beets*		8 to 10	2-3 weeks after
Broccoli		8 to 10	2 weeks before
Brussels Sprouts		16 to 19	3 weeks before
Cabbage		13 to 17	3 weeks before
Carrots*		8 to 10	1-2 weeks after
Cauliflower		8 to 10	2 weeks before
Collards		4 to 6	4 weeks before
Corn*		9 to 12	2 weeks after
Cucumber*		6 to 12	1-2 weeks after
Eggplant		14 to 20	3 weeks after
Lettuce		4 to 7	1-2 weeks after
Greens*		5 to 7	Soon as soil can be worked
Okra		4 to 6	2-4 weeks after
Onion*		8 to 10	2-3 weeks before
Parsley		8 to 10	2 weeks before
Peas*		8 to 10	4-6 weeks before
Peppers		8 to 10	2 weeks after
Potatoes*		10 to 20	2-3 weeks after
Pumpkin*		15 to 18	2-3 weeks after
Radish*		4	3-4 weeks before
Spinach*		6 to 7	3-6 weeks before
Winter Squash*		13 to 22	2 weeks after
Tomato		8 to 12	1 week after
Zucchini*		2 to 4	2 weeks after

Find the Seeds or Seedlings

Now that you have all the information necessary about your preferred vegetables and the companion plants, the step is to identify a right place from where you can purchase your seeds or seedlings. For vegetables that can be directly planted as seeds in the garden, buy from a reputed brand and read the instructions carefully before planting. For those vegetables which cannot thrive when planted as seeds, ensure that you either grow the seedlings to be ready at the right time or buy the ready-made seedlings.

Complete all of the preliminary work well in time for the planting season. Each vegetable will have a "right time" for sowing. Ensure that you know the right time and that you plan accordingly.

Planting Time

Plant your vegetables according to their appropriate time and the map you have drawn for your garden. Your garden should gradually change into the picture you had envisaged when you planned your garden. Add the necessary props where necessary, so the vegetable plants grow well.

For the planting to go well, you will need to have the soil ready, aired, tilled, watered, and fertilized, so when the seedling is planted, everything should work in favor of the plant.

Watering the Plants

It is crucial that the watering is planned well. Your garden needs to be designed in such a way that each plant will receive the amount of water it requires. You could use sprinklers that release the right amount of water at various locations in the garden. Be very careful not to flood the garden, for there is nothing more harmful to the plants than a soaking-wet soil. Not only does it develop root rot, but it also attracts many diseases and pests that love humidity and a dying plant.

Fertilizing the Garden

The garden needs to be fertilized well, so the plants draw their nutrients without depleting all the goodness existing in it. For the plants to grow well, they will need organic fertilizers, and these need to be added every year. Mulching often makes up for these needs, as is planting appropriate companion plants that pull nutrients for themselves and the plants in the vicinity.

For fertilizer, you need to learn to make your compost. Though composting material is available in garden supply stores as well as online stores, the best choice is to make your own. Add the fertilizer as and when it is needed. Do not overload the plant, or you will send the wrong signals to the pests in the vicinity.

How Do I actually Start Companion Planting?

Stage A. Crop Rotation

Treat crop rotation as the very first most essential element of companion planting.

Step 1: Choose plants that grow well in your particular location and soil type. If you have the time, resources and energy, you can alter your soil type. For beginner gardeners, it is better to find plants that suit their current garden soil. It is also a good idea to give some consideration to the following points

A. Ease of access to the site for tending, harvesting

B. Accessibility to gardening tools, compost heap, seating

C. Accessibility to water.

D. The size of beds, borders should be considered. You need to be able to get near to your plants from all sides.

E. Appropriate pathway materials. Bark mulch, paving, decking, gravel, grass are all options. Pathways should ideally be wide enough for a wheelbarrow. If space is limited, you could opt for a few more extensive paths and then have narrow paths coming off the broader paths.

F. Boundaries and windbreaks may also be needed. Fruit bushes could be an option.

Step 2: At this stage, you need to plan your garden layout.

For a reasonably accurate representation of your plans, you could draw your garden layout on graph paper. By using graph paper, you can let each square represent your preferred measurement, e.g., one square = one foot. You can also make allowances for permanent features such as trees or sheds by coloring in the appropriate amount of squares. Now transfer those dimensions represented on the graph paper into your garden. You can use stakes and twine, sand to mark out your scheme. You can also apply those measurements to a raised bed system.

At this stage, you will have decided on the basic layout of your garden and a crop rotation plan. Now it is time to consider adding some diversity to your plant selection.

Step 1: Different Cultivars

Plant different cultivars or go a step further and plant open-pollinated seeds. Open-pollinated seeds will produce plants that are not genetically the same as their parents. Its difference in the genetic make-up could save some of the plants from being destroyed by pest or disease attack.

Step 2: Flowers, Vegetables and Herbs

Add another layer of diversity by combining flowering plants and herbs with vegetable plants. You have several choices. You can create a permanent bed of perennials and bulbs, close to your vegetable beds. Color is always welcome, but you also create a home for beneficial insects.

To make better use of your available space, you could plant flowering plants or herbs between your vegetables. It is a winning combination.

Step 3: Soil Enrichment

It is common sense that plants derive nutrients from the soil, but it is also a fact that some plants give more to the soil than they take away.

Plants such as peas, beans, lentils, alfalfa, LUPINS, soybeans, mesquite and peanuts have an extraordinary relationship with a particular form of bacteria.

The plants named above belong to a group of plants known as legumes, and the particular bacteria are known as rhizobia.

This bacterium grows on the roots of legumes and can trap nitrogen gas and turn it into a form of nitrogen that can help the plant itself and other plants to grow. Some of the nitrogen is used by the plant itself, and when the plant dies, and its roots decompose, more nitrogen is released into the soil. Its nitrogen is then available to plants growing nearby. It does not end there, and if you remove the entire dead plant above and below soil level and then bury all of it back into the soil, it will release more nitrogen, which will boost the crop that is planted in that particular soil.

Many gardeners follow a crop rotation plan that involves growing legumes for two consecutive years and then on the third year growing non-legumes. There is usually sufficient nitrogen in the soil to produce good results.

The process of growing and digging-in legumes is generally referred to as green manure or cover cropping.

Step 4: Repel Bad Insects

We have made use of the ability of one plant to help another in this stage to deal with how one plant can attract/deter insects that may help/damage another plant.

Aromatic plants can release compound which hides the scent of another plant. Because the scent of plant one overpowers the scent off plant two, insects that could damage plant two are unaware of its existence, so they don't attack it. Examples of It process include growing Summer Savory with your bush beans and growing tansy with your potatoes.

Aromatic plants will also deter insects just by the real pungency of their scent. Grow mint with cabbage, garlic with beans and potatoes and basil with tomatoes.

If you have space, you could dedicate an entire bed to these plants, or you could grow individual plants in the same bed as your vegetables.

Step 5: Decoy Plants

Certain insects love individual plants, so we make use of that attraction in two ways.

First, we grow these plants so that the insects are attracted to them. If they are concentrating on these plants, your primary plants are a lot safer.

Second, when we have most of these harmful insects in one location, i.e., on the attractive plant, we can remove that plant and thereby remove a lot of the insects. Just use a bag that is slightly bigger than the plant itself but big enough to drop it quickly over the plant. Drop the bag over the plant and quickly close the bag at the base of the plant. Place your hand at the base of the plant and pull. Now you can destroy/remove plants and insects at the same time.

Examples of decoy plants include growing Black Nightshade to attract Colorado Potato Beatles and growing Nasturtium to attract Aphids.

Step 6: Attract Good Insects

There are several types of insects that you want to attract to your garden. Creating a haven for these will provide you with these beneficial insects.

Provide food and shelter for them, and they will reward you with some great work.

Examples of It process include attracting insects such as spiders and lacewings that will eat cabbage caterpillars, cucumber beetles and aphids.

Stage C: Putting It All Together

Keep a logbook of your efforts during the year. You will need to mix and match. Some combinations will work together, and some won't. Keep a list of combinations in your logbook and record your satisfaction rating.

Knowing what works well this year and what does not work well will save time and money.

Over a few years, you will gather a comprehensive guide to companion planting in general, and specifically for your location.

Companion Plants

Plants for your Garden

All organic gardeners have learned that a diversified garden with a variety of different plants and trees makes for an attractive, healthy one. And I have to add that many experienced gardeners are of the firm belief that certain specific plant combinations even have mysterious, extraordinary powers to assist each other to grow to their full potential. Whether you agree with this or not, scientific studies of companion planting have confirmed the fact that certain combinations do have benefits that are exclusive to those specific combinations.

Lastly, many decades of practical experience in the field have taught gardeners just how to combine specific plants to the benefit of all of them.

Companion buddies assist each other in growing – taller plants will provide cooling shade for shorter, sun-sensitive ones. Its method of planting also makes efficient use of available garden space – while vining plants are covering the ground, the upright ones grow towards the sun so that two very different plants can grow happily in the same plot. Companions help with the prevention of all kinds of pests – strong-smelling plants like garlic and onion will repel insect pests. In contrast, others will lure these insects away from the more delicate seedlings and plants. Individual plants will even attract predators to prey on the pests which attack another plant.

Plants Which Should Always be Grown Together

Garlic and Roses

Seeing that garlic repels pests which attack roses, these two companions have long found themselves together in many gardens all over the world. If you prefer, you can try garlic chives; they are equally valid, and their tiny little white or purple flowers surely make a beautiful picture amongst the roses in spring.

Melons and Marigolds

Nematodes that can occur in the melon roots can be controlled by certain varieties of the marigold plant. Marigolds are maybe even more effective than chemical treatments against It pest.

Nasturtiums and Cucumbers

The vining stems of the nasturtium plant make it an excellent companion for the growing squash and cucumbers in their shared plot. Cucumber beetles are repelled by nasturtiums, and their rambling vines will make sure no beetle comes near your cucumbers. These same vines also make the perfect habitat for ground beetles, spiders and other predatory insects.

Pigweed and Peppers

A study was conducted at the Experimental Station in Coastal Plains in Georgia, which showed that leaf miners prefer ragweed and pigweed to pepper plants. You must remember, though, that you are dealing with a weed, so make sure you carefully remove all the flowers of the pigweed before the seeds setting or they will take over.

Dill and Cabbage

All the plants of the cabbage family like Brussels sprouts or broccoli are pleased to grow together with dill plants. While the floppy, drooping dill is supported by the cabbage, it, in turn, attracts those tiny little beneficial wasps which control cabbage worms and suchlike pests. (Just remember never to try to group dill and carrots).

Beans and Corn

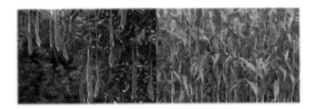

Firstly, bean vines planted to corn stalks have a natural pole against which their vines can climb up. Secondly, the beneficial predators that prey on insects like leaf beetles, leafhoppers and the fall armyworms which attack corn are attracted by the beans.

Tall Flowers and Lettuce

Lettuces like the shade, and this is what tall plants like the flowering tobacco or NICOTIANA, and the spider flower or cleome provide.

Spinach and Radishes

If you plant a few radishes amongst your spinach plants, they will draw the leaf miners to them instead of your precious spinach. You will still be able to harvest radishes since the damage they do is only to the leaves. At the same time, the bulbs continue to grow happily underground.

Sweet Alyssum and Potatoes

This border plant, which is actually (amongst the eighty or so that are even better than fences), with its tiny little flowers, attracts some delicate insects like predatory wasps beneficial to potatoes. Plant alyssum alongside any heavy crops, for example, potatoes. Otherwise, allow it to spread and cover the ground under your broccoli and other arching plants. There is a bonus to planting sweet alyssum; its lovely fragrance will fill your garden with its sweet scent right through the summer.

Dwarf Zinnias and Cauliflower

Beneficial predators like ladybugs are attracted by the nectar of the zinnias. These predators will keep pests away from your cauliflower plants.

Catnip and Collards

Catnip is one of only eight plants that naturally repel mosquitoes. They will also minimize the damage that can be caused by flea beetles to your collards.

Love-in-a-Mist and Strawberries

Beautify your garden by planting a few tall Nigella plants with their pretty blue flowers in the centers of your strawberry rows.

- **Plants Which Should Never Be Planted Together**

The correct combination of plants grown together can be hugely beneficial. Still, also to inform you of those combinations, this should never be planted together. Individual pairs are simply natural enemies and make for unfriendly neighbors. The following is a list of the seven no-go combinations.

Peas and Onions

According to traditional wisdom, it is never a good idea to group peas together with any member belonging to the onion group, and that includes garlic and shallots. The Farmers' Almanac says that beans' and peas' growth will be stunted by the proximity of any onion variety.

Tomatoes and Potatoes

The problem with its combination is that they attract the very same blights. Planting those together means that you are providing a double attraction for the disease, and it will spread a lot easier.

Beans and Peppers

Both beans and peppers are susceptible to a disease called anthracnose, so if you plant them together, the disease will spread quickly from one to the other and destroy your entire crop. Soft dark spots appear on the fruits of the plants and ruin them.

Dill and Carrots

Gardeners all over believe that carrots and dill are fast enemies and should not be planted in combination. However, there are no scientific studies to substantiate this claim.

Grapes and Cabbage

According to folklore, planting your grapevines near your cabbage patch spells trouble; your home-grown grapes and homemade wine will not taste the same. Its unfavorable effect was already known amongst grape growers two thousand years ago, so I tend to believe it.

Tomatoes and Black Walnuts

These trees are quite infamous for being unfriendly neighbors to many a plant. The roots of the tree emit JUGLONE, a chemical toxic to any plants with deep roots, like tomatoes. If you have some of these walnut trees in your garden, you should consider growing your vegetables in raised beds or containers rather than in plots.

Broccoli and Lettuce

In scientific studies, it has been found that lettuce plants are quite sensitive to some of the chemicals left in the broccoli plant residue. I recommend you keep track of where you have grown broccoli before and never try to grow your crop of lettuce in the same spot as their growth and seed germinations could be hindered.

Soil Improvement

Soil groundwork for vegetable development includes a significant number of the standard tasks required for different yields. High seepage is particularly significant for raw vegetables since wet soil hinders advancement.

Sands are significant in developing fresh vegetables since they are more promptly depleted than the heavier soils. Soil seepage achieved by methods for trench or tiles is more alluring than the waste got by planting crops on edges because the abundant water as well as permits air to enter the dirt. Air is fundamental to the development of harvest plants and to particular useful soil creatures making supplements accessible to the plants.

At the point when yields are developed in progression, soil infrequently should be furrowed more than once every year. Furrowing consolidates grass, green-excrement harvests, and yield deposits in the dirt; crushes weeds and creepy crawlies; and improves soil surface and air circulation. Soils for vegetables ought to be genuinely profound. A profundity of six to eight inches (15 to 20 centimeters) is adequate in many soils.

Soil, the board, includes the activity of human judgment in the use of accessible information on crop creation, soil protection, and financial aspects. The executives ought to be coordinated toward delivering the ideal yields with at least work. Control of soil disintegration, support of natural soil issue, the selection of yield revolution, and clean culture are viewed as significant soil-the board rehearses.

Soil disintegration, brought about by water and wind, is an issue in numerous vegetable-developing locales because the topsoil usually is the most extravagant in ripeness and fundamental issue. Soil disintegration by water can be constrained by different techniques. Terracing isolates the land into discrete waste territories, with every territory having its conduit over the patio.

The patio holds the water on the land, permitting it to splash into the dirt and lessening or forestalling gullying. In the forming framework, crops are planted in lines at a similar level over the field. Development continues along with the columns as opposed to all over the slope. Strip trimming comprises of developing yields in restricted strips over an incline, generally on the shape. Soil disintegration by wind can be constrained by the utilization of windbreaks of different sorts, by keeping the dirt all around provided with humus, and by developing spread harvests to hold the dirt when the land isn't involved by different yields.

Support of the fundamental issue substance of the dirt is necessary. The fundamental issue is a wellspring of plant supplements. It is essential for its impact on specific properties of the dirt. Loss of natural issue is the aftereffect of the activity of miniaturized scale living beings that step by step disintegrates it into carbon dioxide. The expansion of excrements and the development of soil-improving harvests are effective methods for providing natural soil issues.

Soil-improving harvests are developed exclusively to set up the dirt for the development of succeeding yields. Green-fertilizer crops, developed mainly for soil improvement, are turned under while still green and ordinarily are developed during a similar period of the year as the vegetable harvests. Spread yields, raised for both soil insurance and improvement, are possibly developed during seasons when vegetable harvests don't possess the land. At the point when a speck of dirt improving harvest is turned under, the different supplements that have added to the development of the yield have come back to the dirt, including an amount of fundamental issue. The two vegetables, those plants, for example, peas and beans having products of the soil framed in pods, and non-legumes are viable soil-improving harvests.

The better the material is at the time it is turned under, the more rapidly it deteriorates. Since dry material breaks down more gradually than green material, it is alluring to turn under soil-improving harvests before they are full-grown, except if extended time is to slip by between the furrowing and the planting of the succeeding yield.

Plant material breaks down most quickly when the dirt is warm and all around provided with dampness. If dirt is dry when a speck of dirt improving harvest is turned under, almost no deterioration will happen until the downpour or water system supplies the critical dampness.

The central advantages gained from crop revolution are the control of sickness and creepy crawlies and the better utilization of the assets of the dirt. Turn is an orderly course of action for the developing of different yields in a pretty much customary succession on similar land.

It contrasts from progression editing in that pivot trimming covers a time of two, three, or more years, while in progression trimming at least two harvests are developed on similar land in one year. In numerous locales, vegetable harvests are developed in revolution with other ranch crops. Most vegetables developed as yearly harvests fit into a four-or five-year pivot plan.

The arrangement of intercropping, or buddy trimming, includes the development of at least two sorts of vegetables on similar land in a similar developing season. One of the vegetables must be a little developing and speedy developing harvest; the other must be bigger and late-developing.

In the act of clean culture, ordinarily followed in vegetable development, the dirt is kept liberated from all contending plants through continuous development and the utilization of defensive covers, or mulches, and weed executioners. In a spotless vegetable field, the chance of assault by bugs and infection INCITANT living beings, for which plant weeds fill in as hosts, is decreased.

Successful administration includes the selection of methods bringing about a consistent progression of the ideal measure of produce over the entire of the regular developing period of the yield. Many vegetables can be developed during the time in absolute atmospheres, even though the yield of land for a given sort of vegetable fluctuates as indicated by the developing season and district where the harvest is created.

1. Atmosphere:

The atmosphere includes the temperature, dampness, sunlight, and wind states of a particular locale. Climatic factors unequivocally influence all stages and procedures of plant development.

2. Temperature:

Temperature prerequisites depend on the base, ideal, and most extreme temperatures during both day and night all through the time of plant development. Prerequisites differ as indicated by the sort and assortment of the particular harvest. The ideal temperature ranges, vegetables might be classed as cool-season or warm-season types. Cool-season vegetables flourish in territories where the mean day by day temperature doesn't transcend 70° F (21° C).

3. Dampness:

The sum and yearly precipitation in a district, particularly during specific times of improvement, had influence neighborhood crops. Water-systems might be required to make up for lacking precipitation. For ideal development and improvement, plants require soil that provisions water just as supplements broke up in the water. Root development decides the degree of a plant's capacity to assimilate water and supplements. In dry soil, root development is incredibly hindered. Very wet soil additionally hinders root development by confining air circulation.

4. Sunlight:

Light is the wellspring of vitality for plants. The reaction of plants to light is reliant upon light force, quality, and every day, or photoperiod. The regular variety in day length influences the development and blooming of certain vegetable harvests.

Continuation of vegetative development, as opposed to early blossom arrangement, is alluring in such harvests as spinach and lettuce.

At the point when planted exceptionally late in the spring, these harvests will, in general, produce blossoms and seeds during the long stretches of summer before they achieve adequate vegetative development to deliver the greatest yields. The base photoperiod required for the development of bulbs in garlic and onion plants varies among assortments, and nearby day length is a deciding component in the determination of assortments.

Certain blends may apply explicit impacts. Lettuce, for the most part, shapes a seed stalk during the long stretches of summer. Yet, the presence of blossoms might be deferred, or even forestalled, by moderately low temperature.

A horrible temperature joined with troublesome dampness conditions may cause the dropping of the buds, blossoms, and little products of the pepper, decreasing the harvest yield. Attractive territories for muskmelon creation are described by low moistness joined with high temperatures. In the creation of seeds of numerous sorts of vegetables, nonappearance of the downpour, or moderately light precipitation, and low dampness during aging, collecting, and relieving of the seeds are significant.

5. Site:

The decision of a site includes such factors as soil and climatic district. What's more, with the proceeded with the pattern toward specialization and automation, generally huge zones are required for business creation and sufficient water flexibly, and transportation offices are fundamental. Geography—that is, the outside of the dirt and its connection to different territories—impacts productivity of activity. In present-day automated cultivating, enormous, moderately level fields take into consideration lower working expenses.

Force hardware might be utilized to adjust geology. However, the expense of such land redesign might be restrictive. The measure of incline impacts the sort of culture conceivable. Fields with a moderate incline ought to form a procedure that may include included cost for the structure of porches and redirection trench. The bearing of a slant may impact the development time of yield or may bring about a dry spell, winter injury, or wind harm.

A level site is commonly generally attractive, albeit a slight slant may help seepage. Uncovered destinations are not reasonable for vegetable cultivating on account of the danger of harm to plants by solid breezes.

The dirt stores mineral supplements and water utilized by plants, just as lodging their foundations. There are two general sorts of soils—mineral and the natural kind called waste or peat. Mineral soils incorporate sandy, loamy, and clayey sorts. Sandy and loamy soils are typically favored for vegetable creation. Soil response and level of ripeness can be dictated by compound examination. The response of the dirt decides as it were, the accessibility of most plant supplements.

The level of corrosive, antacid, or nonpartisan response of dirt is communicated as the pH, with a pH of 7 being impartial, focuses beneath seven being corrosive, and those over seven being basic. The ideal pH extends for plant development differs, starting with one harvest. Dirt can be made progressively acid, or less antacid, by applying corrosive delivering synthetic manure, for example, ammonium sulfate.

Common Mistakes of Companion Planting

Salts

Excessive amounts of salt in your soil can directly affect your plants by damaging or even killing plant roots. Excessive salts can also indirectly affect your plant's health by absorbing water and reducing the amount of water available to plant roots.

Micronutrients

Many other nutrients are essential for healthy plant growth. The difference between these nutrients is the fact that these nutrients are only needed in very small amounts.

However, just because they are only needed in small amounts does not mean that they are not important. For example, a boron deficiency will prevent a plant from growing; a deficiency in iron and manganese will dramatically limit growth.

Because these nutrients are only needed in small amounts, they are referred to as micronutrients. Micronutrients include boron, copper, zinc, iron, manganese, selenium, cobalt, iodine, chromium and lithium. The good news is that it is very easy to ensure that all these vital micronutrients are available for your plants. Quality organic compost will fulfill all your plant's requirements for these micronutrients.

Not Testing your Soil

Do you know just how good your soil is? It might look good, it might feel good, but you have no other clue as to its quality. You need extra information. When you have this information, you can then start to provide an environment in which your plants will thrive. It is the first step you need to undertake.

What Does A Soil Test Reveal?

Your soil test will provide information particular to your soil only. Even within a small locale, the make-up of soil can vary greatly. When you see those wonderful healthy plants in other gardens a few miles down the road, you cannot assume that their soil is the same as yours. Testing your soil tells you what you need to add or subtract from your soil to make it the optimum growing environment for your plants.

Typically a soil test will reveal the following information about your soil.

1. PH

Determining the PH number of your soil will tell you if your soil is acidic or alkaline. It is very important because most plants grow best in soil that is neither too acidic nor too alkaline. They prefer soil that is neutral or only slightly acidic. PH is the scale used for this purpose. The scale ranges from 1.0 (acidic) to 14(alkaline). Ideally, you are looking to get your soil within the range of 6.0 (slightly acidic) to 7.0 (neutral).

A simple way of thinking about this is to think about pure, unadulterated water. Pure water is neutral, 7.0. Depending on what you add to the water, it will then become either more acidic or more alkaline. If you added vinegar to the water, it would become more acidic. If you added ammonia, it would become more alkaline.

Sample pH Scale

0-1 Battery Acid

1-2 Lemon Juice

2-3 Vinegar

3-4 Orange juice

4-5 Tomato juice and rain

5-6 Black coffee

6-7 Milk, urine

7 Pure water

8-9 Seawater

9-10 Baking sodas

10-11 Milk of magnesia

11-12 Ammonia Solution

12-13 Soapy water

13-14 bleach, drain cleaner.

The results of the PH test will reveal information.

2. Levels of Potassium and Phosphorus

Potassium (K)

Potassium is essential for healthy root development, disease resistance and fruit development. The most obvious sign of a potassium deficiency are stunted growth, older leaves look burned, and fruit does not fully develop.

Phosphorous (P)

Phosphorous deficiency results in very poor root growth and fruit development. Phosphorous is not as readily available within the soil as other nutrients, so plants with small root systems, as well as root crops, often struggle to access enough of it. Soils that are very sandy or exposed to strong winds will typically have very little organic matter. It lacks organic matter causes a deficiency of phosphorous.

3. Levels of Magnesium and Calcium

Magnesium (Mg)

Chlorophyll is the substance that gives plants their green color and helps them convert sunlight to energy. Magnesium is a key part of chlorophyll, and a deficiency of Magnesium will mean that the process of converting that sunlight to energy is not working at its most efficient. When this happens, your plants will take their energy supplies from older leaves and send them to newer leaves. The obvious signs of It ailment are when your plant leaves start to dry up and fall off. A magnesium deficiency is a typical problem for acidic, sandy soils.

Calcium

Calcium is vital for the healthy development of plant cell walls. A calcium deficiency will result in very weak growth. Another physical sign of its presence is when your plant leaves start to curl-up and close.

4. Nitrogen

The nitrogen composition of your soil will have a dramatic impact on your plants. Its impact is even more obvious in fruiting plants. Not enough nitrogen will mean that your plants are slow to grow, and growth will be limited. Too much nitrogen will provide you with a lot of growth but not a lot of fruit.

Nitrogen levels in your soil can change from season to season, depending on the amount of organic matter within your soil. As organic matter breaks down, it releases nitrogen that plants can use. To achieve a productive level of nitrogen in your soil, you will need to ensure that you have a consistent level of organic matter in your soil. A generally accepted level of 5% of your soil should be organic matter. The physical signs of a nitrogen deficiency are plants with slow growth and pale leaves.

5. Sulfur (S) and Salts (Na)

Sulfur is essential for the formation of amino acids and proteins in plants. Sulfur is also required by nitrogen if it is to provide food for your plants effectively. All organic matter contains a large amount of sulfur, and this is another good reason for providing an ample amount of organic matter to your soil. Soil that is deficient in organic matter will be deficient in sulfur.

How to Take a Soil Sample

To provide the most accurate results, you will need to take 15 to 20 soil samples from the area you need to be tested. These samples will be mixed to provide a broader general picture of your soil condition. Simply repeat the process outlined below.

a. Get a large plastic bowl, spoon and small trowel or similar.

b. Scrape off loose debris from the top of the soil.

c. Insert spade to a depth of 6 to 8 inches and remove a spade full of soil. Place soil in a plastic bowl.

d. Now remove a few of soil from the side of the hole created by the spade. Place the removed soil in the bowl.

e. Repeat steps A to D until you have removed enough soil to give a good, general representation of your soil.

f. Mix all the collected soil. Remove roots, twigs Mix the soil until no clumps or solids remain. It is now your soil sample for testing.

Some private laboratories provide soil testing facilities, or you can use your local extension office. The following link will take you to a web page that provides both text and clickable links to all cooperative extension offices. As stated earlier, growing conditions can vary greatly from one local area to another.

When you have completed all the formalities, you should receive your results within 4 to 5 weeks.

These results will guide you as regards what to do. Commonly your results will be summarized as low, medium or high. There will be specific details regarding the nutrients described earlier, but in general terms, the following rules apply:

High = a soil that is rich in nutrients and does not need to be altered.

Medium = a soil that is currently nutrient-rich. Currently is the keyword. Everything is fine for the moment, but you will need to amend your soil in time for the following years' growing season.

Low = a soil that is severely lacking in nutrients. It is soil that needs to be amended immediately so that sufficient nutrients are available for your plants.

Excessive = It is a situation that many people fail to think. If your soil contains excessive levels of some nutrients, it will cause an imbalance. Remember, we are looking to get your soil as near to neutral as possible. You will need to either add or remove certain nutrient sources to balance out and get nearer to neutral.

Perfect Combination

Some plants work best with each other, which is why they are considered "perfect combinations." Here are some of that you may want to try yourself.

• Cabbage and Tomatoes. Tomatoes can repel the Diamondback Moth larvae, which are infamous for chewing cabbage leaves and leaving large holes in them.

• Nasturtiums and Cucumbers. Cucumbers make use of Nasturtiums as trellises, while Nasturtiums can repel the dreaded cucumber beetles. They also serve as a natural habitat for ground beetles and spiders, which are predatory insects.

• Ragweed/Pigweed and Peppers. Ragweed and Pigweed are good weeds that can make the soil fertile and can protect plants from being infested by pests.

• Corn and Beans. Its combination has been used for thousands of years, and they are both able to attract beneficial insects such as leaf beetles and leaf horns. Aside from that, they also provide shade and trellis to each other, making sure that they both grow well and become beneficial for humans.

• Dill and Cabbage. They support each other in the sense that dill attracts wasps that eat pests and worms, making sure that the cabbages grow without holes.

• Chives and Roses. Garlic repels the pests that feed on roses, and they also look great when they are planted to each other.

• Tall Flowers and Lettuce. Tall flowers such as Cleomes and NICOTIANA give lettuce shade.

• Sweet Alyssum and Potatoes. Tiny flowers of sweet alyssum attract predatory wasps and also act as a shade for the potatoes.

• Catnip and Collard. They reduce beetle damage.

• Spinach and Radishes. They are both able to repel LEAFMINERS, and radishes can grow safe and well when planted with spinach.

• Dwarf Zinnias and Cauliflower. Dwarf Zinnias are great because their nectar lures predatory insects like ladybugs, and they are known to hunt down and eat common garden pests.

• Melons and Marigold. Marigold repels nematodes just as well as chemical treatments do.

• Love-in-a-mist and Strawberries. They are great for aesthetic purposes.

Here are a couple more companion plants that you can plant in your garden

• Anise. Anise is a good host for predatory wasps, which repels aphids and also camouflages the odor of the other plants to protect them from pests. Anise is best planted with Coriander or Cilantro.

• Amaranth. Amaranth is an annual plant that grows mostly in tropical conditions and is very beneficial when planted near sweet corn stalks. It acts as a shade for the corn, which can moisten the soil and allow corn to grow better and faster. Amaranth also plays host to ground beetles, which are predatory insects who feed on common pests.

• Bay Leaf. Bay leaf repels moths and weevils and can also act as a natural insecticide. Bay leaf is best planted with Tansy, Cayenne Pepper and Peppermint.

• Beets. Beets add minerals to the soil, especially nitrogen, which most plants need to grow. They are great fertilizers for the soil, too, as they contain 25% magnesium and are best planted with melon and corn.

• Bee Balm. When planted with tomatoes, bee balm can improve the growth and flavor of the tomatoes. Bee Balm also attracts bees and butterflies for pollination. She is also great for aesthetic purposes as it always looks good and fresh.

• Buckwheat. Buckwheat is a good cover crop as it is full of calcium and is also able to attract beneficial insects such as butterflies and bees, and repels pests such as aphids, flower bugs, pirate bugs and predatory wasps away. Buckwheat can also provide the soil with phosphorous in which other plants may also be able to benefit.

• Chards. Chards are good not only as vegetables but also as ornamental plants that make pollination possible by attracting beneficial insects. They are best planted with tomatoes, roses, beans, onions and cabbages.

• German Chamomile. It is an annual plant that can improve the flavor of cucumbers, cabbages and onions and also act as host to wasps and hoverflies. German Chamomile also gives soil protection by providing it with sulfur, potassium and calcium and also by increasing oil production in the herbs. Because of increased oil production, more people can benefit from their plants by making different kinds of aromatherapy oils.

• Clover. Clover works as a cover crop or green manure and is best planted near grapevines to attract beneficial insects and make pollination possible. When planted around apple trees, they can repel wooly aphids and also reduce cabbage aphids once planted near cabbages. Clover is also able to increase the number of ground beetles that are great for destroying non-beneficial insects.

• Castor Bean. Castor bean is a poisonous plant that is very effective in repelling moles and mice. And because it is poisonous, you need to be careful where you plant it.

• Chrysanthemums. Fondly called "mums," they can repel nematodes that destroy most plants easily. They are also used as botanical pesticides as they are full of Vitamin C that repels most pests, especially Japanese beetles. They work well with daisies in attracting beneficial insects in fertilizing your garden.

• Comfrey. An underrated plant, Comfrey, is beneficial because it gives calcium and potassium to the soil and also is a good medicinal plant. It also prevents foliage and is a good compost activator, as well as a nutrient miner. It is best planted with avocadoes.

• Costmary. Its flowering plant is very effective in the repulsion and killing of moths.

• Dahlia. While it looks harmless, the dahlia can repel nematodes.

• Four-o-clocks. These flowers can poison the dreaded Japanese beetles. Still, you also have to be careful because being around these flowers too much is also toxic to humans.

• Flax. Flax is used in most diets and is full of linseed oil and tannin that are very useful against the Colorado Potato Bug.

• Hemp. Hemp is very useful when planted near brassicas, as it can repel bugs and pests.

• Hyssop. Hyssop can repel cabbage moths and flea beetles and is best planted with grapes and cabbages. Hyssop is also able to attract bees, which are good for pollination. More often than not, bees make hyssops their homes, which is good for you as this means that your garden will be pollinated even more.

• Horehound. Horehound belongs to the Mint family and can attract beneficial insects such as ICHEUMONID and BRACONOID wasps that consume flies and other insects that feed on your plants.

• LAMIUM. Many gardeners and farmers think that LAMIUM is awesome because it can repel potato bugs which infest most plants and are not good for anyone's garden.

• Lavender. Lavender provides you with great essential oils and is also able to repel non-beneficial insects such as moths and fleas. It is also able to protect plants from whiteflies. Lavender is best planted during the winter season so it could bloom in spring.

- Larkspur. Larkspur can kill Japanese beetles, but you have to be careful around it as it is also poisonous to humans.

- Marjoram. Marjoram can improve the flavor of most fruits and vegetables and also attracts butterflies and bees so that pollination could happen. It's always best to grow sweet marjoram as it gives the best results.

- Morning Glory. Morning Glory attracts hoverflies and also makes the garden more beautiful as it is a vine.

- Stinging Nettles. These plants attract bees and are also full of calcium and silica that are essential for refreshing plants and improving resistance to diseases and also give the soil the nutrients it needs for plants to grow healthy and well.

- Okra. While it is not a vegetable favored by many, Okra is very useful as it gives shade to lettuce, especially during the summer season and prevents the lettuce from wilting. It is also able to protect eggplants and peppers from strong winds. It is also great when planted with peas, cucumber, basil and melons as it also repels aphids away.

- Opal Basil. Opal Basil grows annually and can repel hornworms. It is best planted with oregano, petunia, asparagus and peppers and must be kept away from sage and rue.

- Peach. Peach Trees give shade to asparagus, grapes, onions and garlic and may help repel tree borers and most other pests and insects.

- Hot Peppers. Hot peppers protect most plants' roots from being rotten and provide shelter for smaller plants, especially chili peppers and prevent other plants from being dried up or wilted. It is best planted with okra, green peppers and tomatoes.

- Pennyroyal a great plant that repels fleas, mosquitoes, gnats, flies and ticks.

- PURSLANE. It is a good cover crop for corn and makes the soil healthy and fertile.

141

• Rye. Prevents germs from targeting your plants and is great when planted near tomatoes and broccoli as well as with other vegetables.

• Soybeans. Soybeans provide nitrogen for the soil and also repel Japanese beetles and chinch bugs.

• Turnip. Turnip is also able to provide a lot of nitrogen to the soil and is best planted with peas and cabbage. Do not plant near potatoes, though, as turnip stunts their growth.

• White Geraniums. White Geraniums are effective in repelling Japanese beetles.

The Importance of Compost for Soil Quality

Soil quality plays a massive role in the overall health of your garden. No other single factor is as important. If you have any doubts over the quality of your soil or if you want to stay chemical-free, you need to use compost. Quality compost will provide all the nutrients required for healthy plants. When combined with companion planting, it is the perfect relationship.

Compost improves the condition of soil through altering its biological, physical and chemical properties. Some of the most obvious ways in which compost improves soil conditioning are as follows.

1. It improves soil structure in clay type soil. It improved soil structure results in the clay type soil becoming firmer, more distinct and less prone to clotting. In turn, it leads to better drainage, more nutrients, more aeration and, ultimately, better-growing conditions.

2. It improves the water retention ability of sandy soil by providing a medium in which water can be retained. It results in less rapid loss of water and a more consistent source of liquid for plants. It means that sandy soils are still suitable for plants that do not like to have their roots in water for prolonged periods but that they also have access to water, thus avoiding drought.

3. Compost improves the fertility levels of soil, which in turn means that they need to use chemical fertilizers is greatly reduced or, in some cases, totally removed.

4. Composting your soil increases microbial activity within the soil, which leads to increased resistance to foliar and soil-borne diseases.

5. The increased microbial activity caused by the addition of compost also results in increased efficiency in breaking down pesticides and similar compounds.

6. The addition of compost also reduces the bioavailability of dangerous heavy metals. It is a significant issue when contaminated soils are being reclaimed as healthy soils.

Under normal conditions, organic matter would be broken into small pieces by an army of earthworms, mites, ants, beetles. The resulting organic material would then be further broken down by the presence of fungi, bacterial and protozoa. These microorganisms require certain temperatures to perform optimally.

When we create a compost pile, we are attempting to provide the ideal conditions for the breakdown of organic matter. We do this by providing the following basic components.

1. Organic matter.

2. Minerals.

3. Water.

4. Microorganisms.

5. Oxygen

When all these 'raw materials' come together under certain conditions, we get compost. To make the process even more efficient and faster, we follow certain rules.

When these rules are applied consistently, the result is higher quality compost produced faster than if left to run its natural course of events.

Essential Compost Ingredients

The essential ingredients for quality compost are as listed:

1. Organic matter.

2. Minerals.

3. Water.

4. Microorganisms.

5. Oxygen.

However, providing these ingredients alone will not provide you with quality compost. There is a specific recipe that needs to be followed. Like all good recipes, the result is entirely dependent on using the correct quantities of the correct ingredients correctly. All of the ingredients provided above will determine three important factors.

1. The feedstock. It is the chemical makeup of the raw organic ingredients.

2. The actual physical and shape and size of the feedstock.

3. The population of the microorganisms that is vital to the process.

The Composting Recipe

Bacteria, fungi, microbes, worms and other invertebrates are the workers of the compost pile. It is their work that produces the nutrient-rich compost that plants love. These are the decomposers. Their job is to break down all the materials that we put in the compost pile.

As with any workers, they need to be well-fed. Each one has a preferred diet, and when they all have what they need, the compost pile is working at its most efficient. The trick to making great compost is to provide the ideal conditions for all those decomposer workers to thrive.

Most materials we use in a pile are not ideal for these decomposers. They need a good balance of Carbon (C) and Nitrogen (N) to be efficient. Carbon gives them the energy they need, and Nitrogen gives them the protein they need. Ideally, they prefer a ratio of Carbon to Nitrogen at a rate of 30C: 1N

To give them It ratio and thereby have a healthy compost pile, we need to pay attention to the materials we are using in a pile. The best way to do this is to think of Greens and Browns.

Greens = Nitrogen = Food Scraps, Grass Clippings, Vegetables, Fruit and extensive garden, clear out.

Browns = Carbon = Brown Leaves, Straw, Woodchip, Saw Dust, Newspapers

Maintaining a balance between Greens and Browns also helps with the structural stability of the pile since many of the Green ingredients will be moist or wet, and much of the Brown ingredients will be dry. The Green ingredients do provide necessary moisture content, and the Green helps to prevent the pile from becoming too compacted. Again it is a balance, but It time between moisture retention and air-flow.

Achieving all of the above leaves us with a balance between moisture, air, the carbon and nitrogen provided by the raw materials and the agents of decomposition, i.e., bacteria, insects, fungi, worms, will finish the process.

How is A Compost Pile Layered?

A properly structured and well-managed compost pile can be ready for use within four months in warm temperatures. The structure of the pile is very important, you already know the right ingredients to use, and it is now time to layer them correctly.

The basic structure of a compost pile from bottom to top is a series of layers that begin on a hard surface. You can start your pile on top of pallets, but starting it on a hard surface such as concrete or compacted soil means easier turning. However, using concrete makes it more difficult for beneficial organisms and worms to reach the soil.

My personal preference is to use a suitably sized area and clear it of all grass I then lightly aerate the soil with my fork. It is the best of both worlds. It provides a solid surface that allows you to turn the compost. Still, it allows for quick establishment of contact between worms and the compost pile. Once you have your base ready, it is then time to start building your pile.

Step 1: Place a base layer of materials that will provide carbon like shredded newspapers, dead leaves, wood chips, small twigs and branches. Make them no bigger than 2 to 3 inches in size. Smaller sized materials and greater surface area exposure will speed up the decomposition process. If you have enough materials, you should aim to make this first layer 4 to 6 inches deep. When It layer is in place, you should lightly moisten it.

Step 2: Start your second layer. Its layer consists of nitrogen-rich materials such as grass clippings, fruit and vegetable waste, eggshell, coffee grounds, leftover bread and rice and leafy garden trimmings. If you have access to seaweed, you should use it. Seaweed is an excellent addition to a compost pile. Its layer of nitrogen materials should be 2 to 3 inches deep.

Step 3: You will notice that the first layer of carbon-rich materials was 4 to 6 inches deep and that the second layer of nitrogen-rich materials was 2 to 3 inches deep. It is your ratio guide of approximately two parts carbon to 1 part nitrogen. Try to maintain that approximate ratio by using the thickness of the layers as a guide, i.e., 4 to 6 inches for carbon 2 to 3 inches for nitrogen. Now repeat the process as described in steps 1 and 2.

Step 4: After repeating these layers, your compost pile should now be reaching 4 to 5 feet in height. If you are using a bin, it is time to close it, and if you are using an open compost pile, you should now cover it with plastic.

Step 5: Start a new compost pile using steps 1 to 4.

Step 6: You will need to monitor the moisture content of the pile. Use this sponge test, soak a sponge in water and then squeeze the water out, the moisture content of a wrung-out sponge is approximately the moisture content you are looking for with your compost. You need it moist, not soaking wet. Squeeze a few handfuls of the compost. Ideally, it should yield a few drops of liquid.

If the compost is too wet, grab your fork and turn the compost over. It will allow air in around the compost as well as improve drainage.

If the compost is very dry, you simply need to water it, turn it and water it again. Use the test described earlier to ensure that you do not overwater.

Step 7: Temperature plays a large role in the decomposition process. You will need to check the internal temperature of your compost pile occasionally. You can use your hands or purchase a compost thermometer.

If using your hands, the compost should be hot to touch. If using a thermometer, it should be within the range of 120 to 160.

Check every 2 to 3 weeks. When the temperature starts to decrease, it is time to turn the compost.

Step 8: To turn the compost, you simply need to move the materials from the outside and the top of the compost into the middle and move the middle materials to the outside and top.

It is an easy process if you have a second composting area nearby and ready to go. If not, all you need to do is to grab your fork and dig towards the center of the pile. As you dig, place what you have just removed in a small pile to the side. When you have a significant hole dug into the pile, you just need to start filling the hole with material from the outside of the pile.

When the center is now filled up again, spread the compost you set aside along the top and outer parts of the pile. Inside out, outside in!

Step 9: Wait a few weeks and check the inner temperature again. You are looking for 'hot to touch' or 120 to 160. When your pile reaches this temperature, it will need to be turned one final time.

Step 10: Its stage, you have turned your pile twice, and it is unlikely to heat to those temperatures again. It should start to cool down, so now it is a waiting game. Wait for it to cool down and then give it another 3 to 4 weeks. Timings may vary, but that is the general period involved.

Step 11: Your compost should now be ready to use. It will be a lot smaller than it was originally and will be crumbly in texture. There should not be any significant odor.

Good and Bad Companion

Good Companions

Here is a list of plants that grow well together, with a brief explanation of just why this is the case. Although It list is not by any means an exhaustive list in itself; it only takes a little imagination to bring different species together, when you have the most basic gardening skills. The knowledge that is contained in these notes to guide you.

Asparagus:

Best companions include: Tomato, parsley and Basil; and French marigold planted alongside will deter beetles. If on its own or just with Tomato plants, then Comfrey can be planted around as a good source of nitrogen for both plants.

Beans:

Companions include; Beetroot, cabbage, celery, carrot, cucumber, corn, squash, pea's, potatoes, radish, strawberry.

Beans produce (draw from the air) nitrogen that is beneficial to the other plants

Nasturtium and rosemary can deter bean Beatles, while Marigolds can deter Mexican bean Beatles.

Cabbage Family:

Companions include; cucumber, lettuce, potato, onion, spinach, celery.

Chamomile and garlic can be grown to improve growth and flavor.

Marigolds and Nasturtium can be grown alongside to act as a decoy for butterflies and aphid pests. While mint, rosemary and sage will also deter cabbage moth and ants – as well as improve flavor.

Marigolds planted to carrots attract hoverflies, whose larvae, in turn, eat aphids. The smell of the marigold flowers also confuse the carrot fly

Carrots:

Good companions include beans, peas, onions, lettuce, tomato, and radish.

Including chives in the area will improve flavor and growth. At the same time, onions or leeks will distract the carrot fly by masking the scent of the carrots, as will sage or rosemary.

Celery:

Bean, tomato and cabbage family make good companions for celery.

Nasturtium, chives and garlic deter aphids and other bugs.

Corn:

Good companions are Potato, pumpkin, squash, tomato and cucumber.

French marigold deters beetles and attracts aphids from tomatoes.

Cucumber:

Good companions include cabbage, beans, cucumber, radish, tomato.

Marigold and Nasturtium are good for attracting to themselves, aphids and beetles. Oregano is a good all-round pest deterrent.

Lettuce:

Cabbage, carrot, beet, onion, and strawberry are all good companions for Lettuce.

Chives and garlic discourage aphids.

Melon:

Companions include pumpkin, radish, corn, and squash.

Marigold and Nasturtium deter bugs and beetles as oregano.

Onions:

Good Companions include the cabbage family, beet, tomato, pepper, strawberry, peas, and chard.

Chamomile and summer savory helps improve growth and flavor. Pigweed brings up nutrients from the subsoil and improves conditions for the onions.

Parsley:

Good companions include asparagus, tomato and corn.

Peas:

Good companions include beans, carrot, corn and radish.

Chives and onions help deter aphids as nasturtium.

Planting mint is known to improve the health and flavor of peas.

Peppers:

Tomato, eggplant, carrot and onion are known to be good companions for peppers.

Potatoes:

Good companions include bean, cabbage, squash and peas.

Marigold makes a good general deterrent for beetles, while horseradish planted around the potato patch gives good overall insect protection.

Pumpkin:

Melon eggplant and corn make good companions for pumpkin.

Oregano and Marigold give good all-round insect protection.

Radish:

Companions are carrot, cucumber, bean, pea, melon.

Nasturtium planted around is generally accepted to improve growth and flavor.

Squash:

Companions include melon, pumpkin, squash and tomato, while nasturtium and marigold, along with oregano, helps protect against bugs and beetles.

Strawberry:

Good companions include bean, lettuce, onion and spinach.

Planting thyme around the border deters worms, while borage strengthens general resistance to disease.

Tomatoes:

Good companion plants for tomatoes include; celery, cucumber, asparagus, parsley, pepper and carrot.

Basil and dwarf marigold deter flies and aphids; mint can improve health and all-around flavor.

These are some examples from popular vegetable types and offer a guide as to what to consider for your companion garden.

Bad Companions

There are a few reasons why some plants should not be grown alongside others if you are considering the organic method of growing your vegetables.

I mention particularly organic because the general idea behind companion planting is to avoid the use of chemical pesticides and fertilizers whenever possible.

Some plants should not be grown together simply because they both attract the same pests or other predators, others because they make the same demands on the soil, leading to them both producing a poor harvest. Some plants grown close together may produce a damp environment that leads to fungal or other infections.

Here are some plants to avoid planting close together, if possible, when considering a companion for your veggies.

Beans:

Beans should not be grown in the same vicinity of garlic, shallot or onions as they tend to stunt the growth.

Beets:

Beets should not be grown along with pole beans as they stunt each other's growth.

Cabbage

It is generally thought not to do well near tomatoes, mainly because the tomato plant can shade the cabbage. Avoid planting near radishes, as they do not grow well together.

Carrots:

Avoid planting near dill as this can stunt growth. Dill and carrots both belong in the UMBELLIFERAE family. If allowed to flower, it will cross-pollinate with the carrots.

Avoid planting alongside Celery as this is from the same family.

Corn:

Where possible, avoid planting corn and tomatoes together, as they both attract the same tomato fruit-worm.

Cucumber:

Sage should be avoided near cucumber, as it is generally harmful to the cucumber plant.

Peas:

Onions and garlic stunt the growth of peas.

Potatoes:

Tomatoes and potatoes should not be planted together as they attract the same blight, and use up the same nutrients from the soil.

Radish:

Avoid planting hyssop near radishes.

Make Your Special Mix for Infilling Compost

These are altogether obvious if you manure the incorrect way. Fertilizing the soil the correct way is a straightforward methodology: Simply layer organic materials and a scramble of soil to make a blend that transforms into humus (the best soil manufacturer around!). You would then be able to improve your blossom garden with fertilizer, top dress your grass, feed your developing veggies, and the sky is the limit from there. With these straightforward strides on the most proficient method to compost, you'll have the entirety of the boasting privileges of a star!

Fertilizer

Kinds of Composting

Before you begin heaping on, perceive that there are two kinds of treating the soil: cold and hot. Cold treating the soil is as straightforward as gathering yard waste or taking out the organic materials in your garbage, (for example, foods grown from the ground strips, espresso beans and channels, and eggshells) and afterward corralling them in a heap or canister. Through the span of a year or thereabouts, the material will break down.

Sweltering fertilizing the soil is for the more genuine nursery worker; however, a quicker procedure—you'll get fertilizer in one to a quarter of a year during warm climate. Four fixings are required for quick-cooking hot manure: nitrogen, carbon, air, and water. Together, these things feed microorganisms, which accelerate the procedure of rot. In spring or fall, when nursery squander is plentiful, you can blend one major clump of manure and afterward start a subsequent one while the primary "cooks."

Vermicomposting is made utilizing worm treating the soil. At the point when worms eat your nourishment scraps, they discharge castings, which are wealthy in nitrogen. You can't utilize only any old worms for this, be that as it may—you need REDWORMS (likewise called "red wigglers"). Worms for treating the soil can be bought reasonably on the web or at a nursery provider.

What to Compost

Fertilizing the soil is an incredible method to utilize the things in your cooler that you didn't get to, consequently wiping out waste. Keeping a holder in your kitchen, similar to Its chic white earthenware manure can from World Market, is a simple method to aggregate you're fertilizing the soil materials. If you would prefer not to get one, you can make your own indoor or open-air handcrafted fertilizer container. Gather these materials to begin your manure heap right:

• Organic product scraps

• Vegetable pieces

• Espresso beans

• Eggshells

• Grass and plant clippings

• Destroyed paper

• Straw

• Sawdust from untreated wood

What NOT to Compost

Not exclusively will these things not fill in also in your nursery. However, they can make your fertilizer smell and pull in creatures and vermin. Stay away from these things for an effective manure heap:

• Sick plant materials

- Sawdust or chips from pressure-treated wood

- Pooch or feline defecation

- Weeds that go to seed

- Dairy items

- Manure, grass clippings, leaves

Stage 1: Combine Green and Brown Materials

To make your hot-fertilizer store, hold up until you have enough materials to make a heap at any rate 3 feet down. You are going to need to consolidate your wet, green things with your dry, earthy colored things. "Earthy colored" materials incorporate dried plant materials; fallen leaves; destroyed tree limbs, cardboard, or paper; roughage or straw; and wood shavings, which include carbon. "Green" materials incorporate kitchen scraps and espresso beans, creature excrements (not from pooches or felines), and new plant and grass trimmings, which include nitrogen. For best outcomes, begin fabricating your manure heap by blending three earthy colored with one green material. If your fertilizer heap looks excessively wet and scents, include increasingly earthy colored things or circulate air through more frequently. If you see, it looks very earthy colored and dry, add green things and water to make it somewhat soggy.

Stage 2: Stir Up Your Pile

During the developing season, you ought to furnish the heap with oxygen by turning it once every week with a nursery fork. The best time to turn the manure is the point at which the focal point of the heap feels warm or when a thermometer peruses somewhere in the range of 130 and 150 degrees F. Working up the heap will assist it with cooking quicker and keeps material from getting tangled down and building up a smell. Now, the layers have filled their need to make equivalent measures of green and earthy colored materials all through the heap, so mix all together.

Stage 3: Feeding the Garden

At the point when the fertilizer no longer radiates heat and gets dry, earthy colored, and brittle, it's completely cooked and prepared to take care of to the nursery. Add around 4 to 6 crawls of fertilizer to your bloom beds and into your pots toward the start of each planting season.

Stage 4: Watering the Pile

Try not to include an excessive amount of water; in any case, the microorganisms in your heap will get waterlogged and suffocate. If this occurs, your heap will decay rather than a fertilizer. Screen the temperature of your heap with a thermometer to be certain the materials are appropriately disintegrating. Or, on the other hand, essentially venture into the center of the heap with your hand. Your manure heap should feel warm.

A few gardeners make what's known as manure tea with a portion of their completed fertilizer. It includes permitting full-grown manure to "steep" in water for a few days, then stressing it to use as handcrafted fluid compost.

Each planter is different, so it's dependent upon you to choose which treating the soil strategy best accommodates your lifestyle. Luckily, regardless of which course you pick, fertilizer is extraordinarily simple and naturally cordial. Besides, it's a treat for your nursery. With only a couple of kitchen scraps and some tolerance, you'll have the most joyful nursery conceivable.

How to Grow Healthy Organic Herbs

Herbs are such an awesome blessing from the unstoppable force of life from various perspectives. Their utilizations are many, including culinary, therapeutic, family unit, restorative, and art. Also, their utilizations in the garden as companion plants and many can be utilized as activators in the fertilizer load.

Also, there's no better method to thoroughly enjoy their sharp fragrant characteristics than to grow them directly outside your kitchen entryway.

When you have an herb garden, you will experience passionate feelings for them. Most herbs are genuinely simple to grow. They don't need to occupy a lot of room, Thyme or quite a bit of your time.

Herbs don't experience the ill effects of insects' assault, and they are not inclined to infection issues. Most will endure regardless of whether very dismissed. However, we need our herbs to grow solid and vivaciously to serve us best. So, we should take a look at making the best conditions for your herb garden.

Where to Grow Your Herbs

If you are sufficiently fortunate to have a lot of space for a plot committed to growing herbs, at that point, that is great, a creative and pragmatic approach to grow herbs together is in a winding. I like to interplant herbs all through my garden, exploiting their excellent Companion Planting benefits, just as having the ones I utilize most in the kitchen close by for simple access.

Numerous herbs start from the Mediterranean and incline toward conditions fit to that atmosphere. For example, hot, dry summers and cold, wet winters. Frequently the hotter the summer, the more fragrant the oils of the herb become.

Albeit most herbs will grow in halfway shade, they will grow best if you choose a site with somewhere in the range of 4 and 6 hours of daylight for every day.

Most of the herbs lean toward an all-around depleted soil; however, they will adapt to shifting soil types. You can generally improve your starting soil by including fundamental issues, including manure and mulching. If your soil doesn't deplete well, you should seriously think about structure raised beds or growing your herbs in containers.

Most herbs don't require much in the method for composts. Including fertilizer as mulch with a layer of pea straw or comparative over the top is sufficient to keep most herbs flourishing.

Growing Your Herbs in Containers

Herbs are probably the most straightforward plants to grow in containers. With some idea to the position of the sun, you can grow them effectively on porches, overhangs, patios, and verandas. Along these lines, you can have them at your indirect access – or even in your window ledge.

Container growing is especially helpful if you live in a freezing winter atmosphere, with the goal that you can over-winter your herbs in containers inside.

It's likewise a great method to grow a portion of the herbs you regularly use in case you're leasing. At the point when you leave, you simply take your herb containers with you!

You can choose practically any container to grow herbs in. You could get very creative with your box as long as it has enough seepage and isn't something that may have any dangerous buildup. However, in case you're not too creative, there are custom planters, enormous shallow pots that permit a few types of herbs to grow together, strawberry pots, and window boxes – and I'm sure there are a lot more alternatives.

Littler herbs will be the best decision for container plants. You may be astonished at what number of types of herbs would be upbeat growing together in a similar pot.

Picking moderate growing herbs will imply that you won't need to keep them clean. Clipping what you need for supper will keep them minimized and shaggy. Continuously select sound herbs to give them the best start. Expel any dead or infected leaves to keep them solid.

While preparing them up into their container, recall that they'll be there for some time, so choose a decent, very much depleted preparing mix. Since most herbs don't require a great deal of compost, choose a preparing mix without included manure. Container plants require more thoughtfulness regarding watering needs as they will dry out a lot quicker than plants in the ground. On hot, dry days, you may need to water little containers two times every day.

Occasional Care

Keeping gets rid of your herb garden and watering great during summer are the two fundamental necessities to keeping your set up herbs solid. Mulching will be major assistance with both of these assignments. It will likewise help keep your herb roots cool. Apply a thick layer of mulch – around 3 or 4 inches/8-10 cm to be successful. If you live in a zone with severe winters, you should over-winter a few herbs or treat them as annuals and plant new plants in spring.

Brilliant Oregano

If a portion of your herb plants starts to get, "leggy" trim them practically back to ground level toward the finish of summer. Herbs that will profit by this include oregano, marjoram, all the mints, yarrow, lemon medicine.

A portion of the more bush-like herbs simply needs cutting back to energize rugged growth, for example, rosemary, lemon verbena, and lavender.

What's more, a few herbs ought to be treated as annuals – as such, force them up after the primary growing season and plant new plants growing season. It incorporates basil, dill, chervil, borage, coriander, cumin.

You will profit greatly by remembering herbs for your natural garden. They offer such a lot yet ask pretty much nothing.

A few herbs are best treated as groundcovers; some make superb edging plants; however, I want to grow the majority of my herbs among different plants. They make their mark when their excellence and fragrances can be experienced personally and frequently.

Conclusion: Companion Planting

Thank you for making it to the end of Companion Planting, you can enjoy the benefits of companion planting to make your garden healthier and more productive, and without having to work as hard to repel pests or keep your crops robust. Starting with a solid foundation of healthy soil that is rich in organic matter, carefully plan out how to arrange your companion garden to get the most out of your space.

Remember that increasing yield is not just about spatial efficiency, but also about extending the growing season to be as long as possible. By applying the principles of companion planting, you can have a beautiful, productive garden that takes care of itself. Companion planting is an important way to shift to using more sustainable, organic methods of keeping your garden healthy.

The key to successful companion planting is properly planning where the plants in your garden are going to go. You've got to carefully consider how each of the plants in your garden is going to interact with one another and then place them in the best possible locations to take advantage of those interactions. The biggest limitation regarding companion planting is the knowledge of the gardener. Arm yourself with as much knowledge as possible before you ever put on your gardening gloves.

Keep in mind that one of the most common mistakes that you should never attempt to do is to start big with companion gardening. Even if you have a big lawn or backyard intended for this purpose, you should always try a smaller plot first.

Assess your budget and how much time you want to commit to getting the garden started, and base your decision on that. To maintain a companion garden, you don't need too many materials. A source of water is, of course, essential, whether it is a rain barrel, well pump, or spout. Beyond that, a sturdy spade, a garden rake or hoe, and a trowel are all you need.

Remember that in Companion planting, there are millions of types of insects. Still, not all of them are pests determined to devour your crops. There are a lot of species which are referred to under the umbrella term of 'beneficial insects,' which provide a natural form of pest control. For many gardeners, including myself, they are an essential part of organic and natural gardening.

Once you know which plants you want to grow and what your primary goals for companion planting are, it's time to get your system into action. It book will explain how to get started with companion planting in the real world – taking your plans and making them a reality in your garden.

By weaning your garden off of chemical fertilizers and insecticides, and using natural methods to keep your plants healthy and free of pests, you will be improving not only your plants' health but your own as well. You'll also be improving the environmental and carbon footprints. And your garden will be more robust as a result and better equipped to handle various weather conditions, droughts, and disease. Good luck!

HYDROPONIC GARDENING SECRET:

THE COMPLETE BEGINNERS GUIDE TO LEARN HOW TO MAKE YOUR HYDROPONIC SYSTEM FROM SCRATCH.BUILD YOUR SUSTAINABLE GARDEN, GROW VEGETABLES, FRUITS & HERBS EASILY WITHOUT SOIL.

BY EDWARD GREEN

HYDROPONIC

GARDENING

Secret

THE COMPLETE BEGINNERS GUIDE TO LEARN HOW TO MAKE
YOUR HYDROPONIC SYSTEM FROM SCRATCH.
BUILD YOUR SUSTAINABLE GARDEN, GROW VEGETABLES,
FRUITS & HERBS EASILY WITHOUT SOIL

EDWARD GREEN

Introduction: Hydroponic Gardening Secret

In the nineteenth century, there was not a lot of forwarding movement in the idea of hydroponics except for research into the types of nutrients that plants needed to sustain life when grown in water. After the first ideas were published, other scientists took up the study, even going so far as to the necessary ratios of the minerals and vitamins that would need to be added to the water the plants grew in.

While foreign explorers took the word of hydroponics back to their native lands, the everyday use of hydroponics began in the twentieth century with scientific analysis. In the early years of this century, there was a renewed interest in finding new methods for growing and sustaining plant life. Interest grew during World War II when it was found that shipping food to American troops stationed all around the world was expensive. It prompted new experimentation with the use of hydroponics to provide crops grown economically to the soldiers. It caused a general increase in the overall popularity of the use of hydroponics.

Much of the formulations for the solutions of nutrients used in hydroponics gardening were formed during this time. One crucial experiment that shows the practical use of hydroponics gardening took place on a little island in the Pacific Ocean called Wake Island, which was used as a rest stop and refueling station for planes flying from the United States to Asia. Hydroponic gardens were used on the island to provide fresh food to the travelers and crew members of the flights that stopped there.

There was one crucial invention in the 1950s that led a marvelous boost to hydroponic gardening, and that was plastic where before greenhouse beds had been made of concrete with water lines made of lead pipe. Now everything could be made from plastics. And the plastic pipes did not rust or burst like the lead pipes often did. And using plastic for hydroponic gardening allowed for the use of water reservoirs, filters, improved irrigation, and drip systems. The drip system, especially, is still widely in use today because it is practical, easy to use, and inexpensive.

Is hydroponics complicated?

Hydroponics is extremely simple, and it certainly is not rocket science. Usually, people tend to have a preconceived notion that hydroponics is complicated, like scientific experiments or lab experiments in which tubes, meters, gauges, and troughs are used. However, hydroponics is an easy practice you can use to start growing plants immediately. Once the system is in place, you merely need to choose the plants you want to grow and get started. While doing this, ensure that you are measuring the nutrients required by the plants meticulously and can cater to the water requirements of the plants. There are various premix nutrients available these days, and it certainly makes the job easier.

Is the produce watery and tasteless?

All those who are skeptical of hydroponics often claim that the plants grown using this method tend to have a strong flavor of chemicals and are tasteless. These claims are entirely baseless, and it is impossible to distinguish between the plants grown using conventional methods and the ones grown through hydroponics. The nutrient a plant absorbs is the only condition upon which the taste and flavor of the fruit or vegetable depend on. As long as the ideal nutrients are provided to the plants, the products will not be watery or tasteless. You have all the control over nutrients a plant absorbs. Therefore, you can quickly increase the nutritional value and the flavor of the produce.

Is hydroponics expensive?

Setting up a hydroponic system might be the only upfront cost involved. However, the various benefits you stand to gain from this method of growing plants provide significant returns on the investment you make. You can further reduce the costs by making the hydroponics system at home. All the hydroponics systems can be effectively built for less than $150. All it requires is time and plenty of patience. Another popular misconception is that using high-intensity bulbs in the grow rooms can increase your electricity bill rather drastically. However, all the high-intensity bulbs used in grow rooms are incredibly cost-effective.

Is hydroponics only for indoors?

Growing plants in a controlled environment are the primary objective of hydroponics. As long as you can control the environment, you can grow plants indoors or outdoors. If you want to grow plants outdoors, then they must be grown in greenhouses, and it is the most commonly used method for commercial hydroponic enterprises.

Are chemicals used in hydroponics?

It is a common question a lot of beginners tend to have about hydroponics. The most common nutrient mixture for hydroponics includes nitrogen, oxygen, and air. To this mixture, potassium, phosphorus, and nitrogen are added, along with other trace elements. Before you start worrying about all this, stop for a second and think about a simple fact that the entire universe is made of chemicals in one form or the other. You don't have to depend on pesticides or other fertilizers for increasing the yield of plants as long as the nutrient solution you provide the plants is sufficient. Then, you have nothing to worry at all. When you think about it, most of the products available on the market these days are grown in soil that is filled with inorganic fertilizers that help improve the overall yield. The output might increase, but the soil gets severely damaged in this process. Apart from it, all the fertilizers used in conventional cultivation are washed away by rains, and they directly drain into the ground and underground natural water resources. Too much fertilization of water bodies leads to environmental pollution.

Is hydroponics profitable?

Hydroponics has been receiving plenty of media attention and is steadily growing in popularity. That said, a lot of people still wonder whether it is commercially viable or not. Evidence does suggest that hydroponics is commercially viable. Initially, hydroponic farming was considered to be extremely expensive because of elevated overhead costs. However, specific steps can be taken to reduce the costs involved. The LED lighting technology, coupled with a stacked rack system, helps reduce the costs of essential overheads, such as space and light. Investing in high-yielding crops with shorter growth cycles is also a great idea.

Is the food grown hydroponically healthy?

The health of a plant in hydroponics depends on the nutrient solution used. When the plant receives all the nutrients it requires to grow efficiently, the food produced will be as nutritious as, if not more, than the one grown in soil. While using hydroponics, you don't have to spray the plants with pesticides commonly used for keeping soil-borne pests away. Therefore, it increases the quality of the produce. Apart from it, the nutrient value of the food produced can also be increased by altering the nutrient solution. Since you have complete control over all of this, the food grown hydroponically is certainly quite healthy.

The Science behind Hydroponics and How It Works

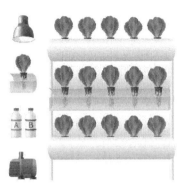

Hydroponic gardening is like fun and a hobby, and it is good to see your crops growing healthy and beautiful. However, to get a good crop, you need to understand the science behind hydroponic systems. It is not as simple as gardening in soil. To achieve good results, you will need to learn the system thoroughly.

Three essential components are required for a plant to grow; these are water, air and soil. Out of these three, water is the essential element for the growth of plants. It transports the essential nutrients, salts and sugars to the cells in the different parts of the plant. The natural environment and soil in which a plant grows may not be perfect. Hence, in traditional farming, plants may not show the growth results to their full potential. However, in hydroponics, an ideally perfect artificial environment is provided. The water is continuously provided with nutrients required for the plant's growth, which the roots of the plant absorb.

This solution of water with essential nutrients is known as 'nutrient solution.'

This nutrient solution is provided through a human-made embedded system. Its system is created in such a way that the evaporation of the solution is less. Therefore, the nutrient-rich water is always available to the system. You may already be practicing the hydroponic system if you have put flowers in a vase with water.

The main principle of hydroponics is that soil provides support to the plant and all the essential nutrients and minerals that are required for its growth. But during research, it was discovered that plants could also absorb required nutrients from liquid mediums or solutions.

Today, plastic reservoirs are used for most of the hydroponic techniques. However, other materials can also be used for making the reservoir, like concrete, vegetable solids, wood and metal. The containers should exclude the light; otherwise, the nutrient solution will grow algae and fungus. The containers are needed to be covered to prevent evaporation of the water solution.

The essential elements of a simple hydroponic system are:

Nutrient Solution: It is the solution of essential nutrients, water and oxygen supply. It comes directly in contact with the roots of plants in the hydroponic system.

Plant Holding Material: It is the base in which cups are placed. These cups contain holes to supply essential nutrients.

Substrates: In traditional farming, soil holds the plant firmly for growth, but in hydroponics, the soil is not used. That's why substrates like sand, coconut fiber, rice husk and volcanic stones are used.

Oxygen Supply: Each plant needs an oxygen supply for their growth. In the hydroponic system, oxygen is supplied by a simple mechanism.

What kind of crop should be chosen?

You should be careful while choosing crops for hydroponic gardening as this system is not designed for large scale farming. Consider the following points:

1. Choose a crop that does not occupy a large area per plant.

2. Choose fast-growing crops, which may take around 3 to 4 months or less to grow.

3. Crops that take a longer time to grow should be those that continue to yield over a particular time.

4. Choose crops that do not have full canopy as it can prevent others from getting enough sunlight. It will enable you to have a variety of crops.

How it Works

Factors Required

The following factors are essential for the success of crop growth.

1. Water

Water is an essential part of a hydroponic system. Without water, no hydroponic system will exist. To prepare a solution culture, you can use regular tap water. A PPM meter can be used to know the density of salts, minerals in the water. You can get a PPM meter online quickly. The water containing 200 to 300 PPM is considered soft. Once the water is free from any harmful chemicals, you can use it in your hydroponic system.

If the PPM measure is above 300 ppm, the water is considered hard and is usually rich in magnesium and calcium. These two elements are essential for a plant's growth, but too many of them will cause deficiencies. They will disturb the balance of nutrient solution. To use such water, you should either filter it or dilute it with distilled water.

2. Distilled Water

Distilled water is free of minerals. If you add this to your nutrient solution, it doesn't disturb the balance of nutrients. An acidic environment is required for a plant's growth, and distilled water's pH value is neutral. It does not provide the required acidity.

3. PH

The PH level of water is more important in defining a plant's growth. If the pH level is correct, the plant will flourish. Still, an incorrect pH level may lead to deficiencies in the plant's growth, and if not corrected, a plant may die. PH level of water is very prone to fluctuations when compared to soil. For beginners, it may be an enormous headache as they don't know how much is required to add. Initially, gardeners would have to measure, adjust and repeat the process to reach the required pH level.

PH level also changes when the plant starts to sip the nutrients, and therefore, it becomes necessary to check the pH level every morning.

4. Oxygen

We know that plants use carbon dioxide and release oxygen. But carbon dioxide is absorbed by the upper part of the plant. The roots can't use photosynthesis as they are below the ground, and they use the required energy transported from the leaves. In soil, roots can receive oxygen from the tiny air pockets, but in water, if you drown them, plants will die.

Drowning the plant's roots is not merely dipped in water, and different methods are used.

5. Nutrient Solution

In traditional gardening, plants get the required nutrients from the soil. In hydroponics, these nutrients are supplied by the nutrient solution. Fourteen nutrients are essential for a plant's growth, and water doesn't have all these. Also, the requirements of these nutrients change frequently as the plant grows and hence, you cannot stick to a single composition of solution throughout the growth. Different plants require different ratios of nutrients for their growth.

You can buy readymade nutrient solutions from hydroponics stores, and their ratios are printed on their labels, for example, 2-1-6, 0-5-4, and 5-0-1. These ratios are usually NPK, i.e., Nitrogen (N), Phosphorus (P), and Potassium (K). These are usually called ratios, but in fact, these are the percentages of each macronutrient in the solution. It means, if the label has 0-5-4 printed, it stands for 0% Nitrogen, 5% Phosphorus, and 4% Potassium.

Hydroponics vs. Aquaponics

Hydroponics

We have already said several times that the advantages of using a hydroponic system certainly concern reduced maintenance, the possibility of cultivating at any time of the year, and the opportunity to control the climate of the cultivation environment. More generally, the great advantage of hydroponics is in complete control over nutrients and, therefore, on the growth of plants. Furthermore, hydroponically grown plants perform better than plants grown in the soil. Many systems of this type recycle water and reduce waste.

These soil-free cultivation systems use only 10% of the amount of water needed for conventional crops. They are reasonably easy to build and assemble. Hydroponic gardens do not require the use of herbicides or pesticides, precisely because weeds do not grow there, they need little space. They do not depend on the growing seasons, because they use lamplight, which can be installed anywhere.

However, hydroponic gardens have some cons; for example, if the temperature is too high or too low, even for a single day, the plants could die or otherwise suffer severe damage. Also, the purchase of hydroponic systems and accessories may require a significant expense, especially if you are not an expert.

Aquaponics

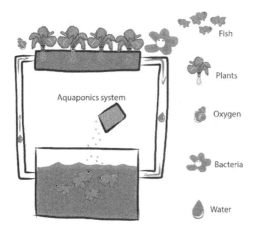

Aquaponics system

Fish

Plants

Oxygen

Bacteria

Water

With an AQUAPONICS system, it is possible to use 1/10 of the amount of water generally used for the irrigation of traditional crops in soil: even less water than the quantities used in hydroponic cultivation. Furthermore, being a natural ecosystem, it is not possible to use harmful petrochemical products, pesticides, or herbicides.

To feed it and make it work, feed the fish in the system and collect the plants that will develop.

Among the advantages offered by this type of system, there is undoubtedly great freedom in choosing the place; in fact, it is possible to grow anywhere: at home or in a garage, in a greenhouse, or in a courtyard to be set up as you prefer. But there is more because everything is scalable. Based on the available budget, it is possible to choose the size and space to be dedicated to this type of system, which can be expanded.

AQUAPONICS offers the possibility of growing anywhere, even vertically, and thus producing a large quantity of food in minimal space. In tower AQUAPONICS systems - for example - the plants are stacked on each other; the water comes down from the top of the tower and reaches the roots and then falls directly into the fish tank.

Among the ideal cultivation systems for AQUAPONICS, there is undoubtedly the DWC (deep water culture), which provides a large cultivation container, low and wide, which floats in a channel full of water from fish and appropriately filtered to remove the solid waste. The plants are placed in unique holes created within the cultivation plan; here, the roots of the plants are free and in contact with the underlying water. Its method is ideal for growing salads and other vegetables that snowball and don't need large quantities of nutrients.

Another system widely used in AQUAPONICS cultivation is the TFT (Nutrient film Technique), which provides for the presence of a slightly inclined tank on the bottom of which mat rich in nutrients is applied.

Water flows inside the tank, which takes the nutrients from the film placed on the bottom and distributes them to the roots of the plants that directly touch the water flow.

The plants are arranged inside holes made in a tube placed above the inclined tank: in this way, the roots hang freely in this continuous flow of water. It cultivation method works very well for plants that need little support, such as strawberries and broad-leaved vegetables, for example.

The NFT system is also a great way to develop crops vertically and use unused space because it can be hung from the ceiling above other crops.

How does AQUAPONICS work?

AQUAPONICS effectively transforms the cultivation plant into a small, utterly autonomous ecosystem, in which water is continuously recovered, and waste is recycled from the roots.

The combination of water, fish, and plants represents the ideal opportunity to discover, deepen, and convey the importance of self-sufficiency and sustainability. The AQUAPONICS cultivation system is characterized by a recirculation system, where the water - with the help of suitable pumps - is taken from the tank where the fishes are

179

located and conveyed into a filter, which carries out the nitrification process, bringing the formation of nitrite and nitrate destined to be assimilated by plants.

In essence, the water collects and transports all the liquid. Solid waste naturally produced by fish (which without polluting it pollutes the environment), and the system filters them thanks to the help of beneficial bacteria, which transform them into nutrients. At this point, the now purified nutrient solution returns to the plants' disposal, to guarantee them the right nutrients, and then is put back into the fish breeding tank, thus closing the cycle. In this way, the waste is eliminated, and the plants get the right amount of nutrients without the need for additional nutrients.

Which plants can be grown with AQUAPONICS?

The varieties of plants that can be grown with the AQUAPONICS method are many, potentially all; in particular, all those that do not need specialized supports to grow, including broad-leaved vegetables, salads, and aromatic herbs.

What fish for AQUAPONICS?

As for the fish that can be used within an aquaculture system, it is possible to choose any freshwater fish, including prawns. Of course, depending on the type of fish chosen, it is necessary to set the system differently, based on the characteristics of the variables selected, to ensure the right amount and type of nutrients for the plants.

What do you need to create an Aquaculture facility?

Aquaculture plant from scratch, it is necessary to purchase a tank intended for breeding fish, a hydroponic tank equipped with a pump - which will be positioned above that of the fish - in which plants will be placed. These bacteria allow the decomposition of the waste of the fish, filters, a kit to measure and adjust the pH, supplements to solve any problems and nutritional deficiencies and then, of course, the fish you prefer and the plants to grow.

Aquaculture with serenity, it is advisable to purchase a system and ready-to-use kits, which will only need to be assembled and set up following the instructions on the package.

In general, the start-up and maintenance of an AQUAPONICS system do not require great care and attention, but - like all crops of this type, including hydroponics and AQUAPONICS - it requires some checks, such as adequate temperature, pH, humidity, correct ventilation and aeration, surface cleaning and the right amount of nutrients (therefore the correct number of fish).

One of the crucial aspects to consider at the beginning is precisely the relationship - which must be well balanced - between the number and type of plants chosen and the number and breed of fish you wish to breed.

In this way, you can guarantee a healthy and efficient environment.

The other factor to always keep in mind is the nourishment provided to the fish, which must be highly qualitative and supplied in the right doses to guarantee the balance of the environment.

Choosing   the   Right   Hydroponic   System

There are different types of hydroponic systems, choosing which is best suitable might seem a little difficult, especially when they all have appealing benefits. Listed below are the different types of hydroponics;

- Drip system
- Nutrient film technique
- Water culture
- Ebb-flow

Drip System

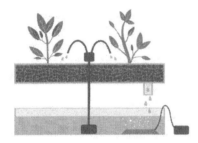

It is a prevalent method, and it is quite similar to the NFT plant system. The plants that are on the drip system will be placed in a table that is slanted; this will help to direct the nutrient solution that has overflowed into the recovery system. The recovery drip system is where the solution that is not taken up by the plant goes back into the reservoir. The water that goes to the no recovery system is taken as wastewater.

This drip system has a drip line, and a submersible pump controls it, and this supplies a nutrient solution to the base of every plant that grows in the media. Different growth media is used in these techniques, and these are the clay, pebbles, and stone wool. Stone Wool will allow the farmers to flood the media less frequently; this is because they tend to hold more moisture that would help keep the plant nutrient intake intact, unlike other growth media. However, in cases where the drip is more constant, then clay pebbles make it quite easier to manage nutrients.

The drip system is quite more accessible and affordable, and this has made it famous by many persons who want to engage the hydroponic system. It has an adequate way of controlling the way plants are fed. However, they are also prone to pH and EC fluctuations. One of the main goals of the hydroponic system is to achieve an automated system, and then with all the plug and play tools, we have around today.

Nutrient Film Technique

Several hydroponic systems are usually hybrids, and this particular system is not different. However, this is quite complicated as the set-up would require a lot more experience and skill to be able to set-up. However, the result of the Nutrient Film Technique is usually better than another system for hydroponics.

All other systems are cold, but their challenges usually result from one of all these three things; water, air, and nutrients. Hence the beauty of the NFT; doesn't have any of these challenges. All the three elements needed for the growth of the crop are all available all the time; Water, Air, and Nutrients. In this present time, several persons see the NFT as a hollowed cut out, where there is a cylindrical tube that runs down a downward slope. Then it houses the parts that carry the nutrient and water. The plants are spaced in a proportion, and then it is placed in the holes on the upper surface of the tube. The use of growing media is not necessary, and just like the AEROPONICS, the growers can use collars to hold the plants in place.

The nutrient productive solution is pushed into the reservoir, which is directly located at the bottom of the channel, and this is directed to the highest part of the channels and made to flow continuously downstream via the roots. The water that is not used will be made to drain inside the back through the reservoir for recirculation. However, if NEFT is appropriately arranged, it is taken as the best in the class of hydroponic systems. However, paying attention and setting all the details is something that can only come from experience and skill.

Water Culture

Some types of water culture are quite very similar to the ebb and flow systems. But their operation is practically not the same as the ebb and flow. The typical water culture will consist of vessels that are always flooded, but this time around, it is never drained. The plant would continue to float around and in the water in the Styrofoam rafts. They may also be held in the net pots, and these pots are kept directly above the waters, and then the roots are suspended in the water below. Its process is usually referred to as the deep water culture. The plants are then exposed to the nutrient-rich medium all the time. However, to prevent the plant from suffocating, the water should be adequately oxygenated with air stones or air pumps.

One of the advantages of this water culture is the ability to run the nutrient solution for the plan at a much lower concentration. Since the food source is always present and the plants are free to feed when they need, hence there is a good chance of an excellent yield.

The disadvantage is that, since the roots are always in the solution, then whatever is in the solution, whether it is good or bad, will increase, and this is a severe threat to

PYTHIUM and FUSARIUM. However, the addition of HYPOCHLOROUS acid will stop the development of any water-borne diseases.

The Ebb and Flow system

This particular system is well recognized as one of the traditional hydroponic systems. It is because it has some unique advantages and functions. The ebb and flow system usually consists of a shallow table, and this comes with a centralized flood with a drain system also. It drains system is hooked to a set of timers which are used to control the feed schedule. The system also has a valve that is used to control the overflow, and this is installed so that it can control the height of the water that is placed on the tray to hold the plants.

As soon as the plant tray is flooded for the duration of time, the water will be removed from the tray into the reservoir system; this reservoir is placed under the table. There are lots of benefits that are seen when this system of hydroponic is chosen. It includes the ability to carry plants about if they are eventually crowded; also, it is straightforward to set up, and you could customize the system based on the spatial and another form of limitations.

With this system too, if you go out leaving your plants to be somewhere else if you do not return on time, then you lose all your plants in a matter of hours. However, some plants can be very resilient; hence, if you open the system and you notice that the plants are becoming wilted, then you can try to bring them back by watering them immediately; they may want to make you happy again.

Factors to Consider When Choosing the Best Hydroponic System

Gardening nowadays can be advantageous and fun, especially when it is practiced in the right manner. It will not only save you the stress, but it will also add to the beauty of your compound.

The market is currently filled with lots of hydroponic systems, and these kits are sometimes complicated to choose from, as many persons who make gardens find it quite challenging to choose the right hydroponic system.

Available Space:

Firstly you need to check the space that is available and how far you will be willing to create and install the hydroponic system. It is quite important because the available space will affect the number of buckets and pots that can be installed in the hydroponic system. It will then affect the plants that will be grown on the site.

In several cases, small hydroponic systems will need as much as 16 square feet on the floor space. You will also need to have some extra space that will be needed to hold the water reservoir. There is also space needed for the lighting, coolers, and pump.

Automation

There are lots of components that are used in the hydroponic system. These components include the pumps, lights, and some other essential components. These components are quite crucial in ensuring that the systems are highly automated. Automation is also an option for you to decide. There are both manual and automatic systems, and it is your responsibility to choose.

Different recent researches have indicated that gardening failure that happens usually happens because of the reduced temperature control and the levels of water. Hence getting a system that could be automated will do half of the work done. The decidedly more modern systems usually come with electronic devices that can automatically check and regulate temperature, humidity, and water levels. Thus this takes half of the work from you.

Expandability:

As a person who wants to begin hydroponics, you may want to start with a smaller kit. Then if it becomes favorable, you will want to expand your gardening. As soon as you convince yourself of the benefits of having a hydroponic farm, then you will want to increase the scope of the system so that you can benefit more.

In cases where you want to expand, then you will need to have functional space so you can hold additional buckets or pots so that you can effectively hold other plants.

Its factor determines the output, and it is a crucial factor that can help you make an outstanding choice for the system.

Energy efficiency

Every hydroponic system that you choose uses electricity, and this supports the pumping, lighting, and the air. The cost of electricity can be a high burden, especially when the materials that are used are not energy friendly. Using energy-saving LED bulbs can be better. A better spectrum of light is what is required for the system to come out in the best condition for the plant.

Hence when you purchase your hydroponics system, you should ensure that you are getting the energy-saving LED bulbs as this will go a long way to reduce the expenses that come with operating the system.

System price and the cost to set-up:

There are different costs to set up the different types of hydroponic systems, and this can be another factor that can affect your choice. They can be bought as already built, and you can also construct one yourself. Constructing yourself will make you need a professional, and this can affect your cost because if you do not have any idea how to make it, then you will hire a professional to help you construct. It can be quite expensive for those beginning, and it will need proper monitoring, especially during installation.

Crops:

The crops you are going to be planting should also be factored in, as this can affect the system you are going to use. What is the optimum temperature of the crops you want to grow, and also, you have to consider if the crops are small or large stature? A crop that is quite large when it is matured will need to be grown on a hydroponic that can hold it firmly. It, therefore, means that AEROPONICS is not the best option for this kind of crop since it doesn't have a firm media for it.

Facility:

You should consider the layout, utilities, and all the environmental factors. You will have to check if you will need to work with pillars, small rooms; also, you will need to be in a facility that can deal with fluctuation in temperature.

Also, you can check the labor and how efficient you want your labor to be. Consider how many persons you want to be in the facility.

Equipment

Keep in mind that most of this equipment is widely available and can come in many different forms. Some of this equipment is available to you at lower prices or higher prices. Some of the equipment may be sold by many different brands at different price points, or they may offer you very different features on top of the primary function of the device or equipment.

Reservoir

The first piece of equipment is going to be the most fundamental piece of equipment that you will use. It is your reservoir. The reservoir is going to hold all of the nutrient solutions that you make, meaning that you will need this to ensure that, ultimately, your plants will get the nutrient solution that they are going to need. However, if you are low on money, many people find that they have great luck using 5-gallon buckets that are typically used for paint or cat litter, or even those big, 20-gallon plastic storage bins that you can buy at the store relatively cheaply.

When you decide how big your system is going to be, or how big of a reservoir that you will need, you need to keep the following guidelines in mind:

- ½ gallon of water for every small plant on the system

- 1 ½ gallon of water for every medium plant on the system

- 2 ½ gallons of water for every large plant on the system

It is a bare minimum. Many people like to double this volume just to make sure that they need to fine-tune it always. However, in remembering this rule, you will make sure that your plants will have enough water and nutrients. It means that you know that you are giving them what they need to thrive.

Growing Tray

The growing tray is going to be mostly dependent upon your reservoir and your system of choice. However, just about anything that will hold your plants will work for this. If you are using a plastic bucket and a deep water culture, you could get by with just using holes cut into the tops of the bucket to allow for netting pots to sit into them.

To help yourself choose the proper growing tray, consider the following:

•How much space do you have?

•How deep do you need it?

•How widely apart do your plants need to be?

•Which system are you using?

•How are you going to connect it to the reservoir?

Air Pump

Air pumps are crucial if you make use of a deep water method. Some others may also opt to use them, but the only system that requires them is the DWC. When you are choosing your air pump, make sure that, along with it, you also choose out the right tubing. The air pump is going to require both of those to be able to aerate the tank properly.

When you are going to choose an air pump, all you have to do is make sure that it will get the job done. However, that does not require very much, and often, people will make use of the aquarium air pumps that you can buy at just about any fish store. If you can buy a pump there, you will find that ultimately, you will be able to get the proper aeration.

Water Pump

The water pump is going to be much more particular to the system that you buy. Because nearly every system will involve a pump to some degree, you are going to want to ensure that this will work properly. You need to have a reliable water pump, no matter which kind you choose. Think of the pump as the heart of your system—it is going to pump the life-giving nutrient solution to all of the plants to sustain them all. Without the pump, your system runs the risk of dying, and because of that, you want to ensure that it is always reliable.

Lighting

Lighting is an essential point to consider, as well. You must be able to provide your systems with the appropriate lighting for the plants that you have chosen if you hope to be able to keep them alive. Remember that you must always check the lighting requirements for your plants before planting them so you are aware of what they will need.

Timer

A timer is another crucial point of most well-regulated systems. When you are considering a timer for your system, you are going to need to decide how many systems you want your timer to be able to handle. Some timers can be programmed to have very different speeds and activation times for them. Some timers can be programmed to manage your entire system, allowing you to plug several different pieces of equipment onto them and have them run on different schedules. Others, however, will be very simplistic.

Growing Medium

The growing medium can be chosen with plenty of flexibility. Many different methods can be used depending on your preference, as well as the preference of the plants that you are growing. Some may require more absorbent mediums to allow for water to be held where it needs to go. In contrast, others may want equipment that will simply allow the nutrient solution to flow freely. Some systems may choose to skip it entirely.

Let's go over the most common growing mediums that you are going to find in a hydroponic setup:

•**Rock wool:** This is perhaps the most common one in terms of versatility. While waiting for the seeds to sprout, you can use them when you decide to clone your plant. You can use it for just about any system, and it will work well.

•**Oasis cubes:** These are also used very commonly when using hydroponic systems. Oasis cubes are neutralized already and can retain water whenever they need to.

•**Coconut husks:** Commonly referred to as coco coir, this material comes from processing the husk of a coconut. You may either chip it into pieces that look much like the wood chips that you would see on older playgrounds. You may also see fibers, where it has been broken down more.

•**Rock:** Some people will simply use rocks or gravel when they need a growing medium. It is free—you can get them just about anywhere outside. However, it is a good idea to remember to keep the rocks that you use smooth, so they do not damage roots. You must always remember that you also need to ensure that you sanitize them before adding them to your system.

•**Expanded clay:** Some people like to use expanded clay—this is a neutral form of medium that can be used much like rocks. It is essentially some clay that has been heat-treated until it popped and became porous. You can reuse it by sanitizing and continuing to make use of it in the future.

•**Perlite and vermiculite:** These are two prevalent rocks that are treated much like expanded clay—they are heated until they pop to allow them to be incredibly lightweight and versatile. They are typically mixed, as perlite is usually lighter and will float.

Net Pots

Net pots are tiny cups that most seedlings are grown in. They are the tiny, plastic cups with the holes in them that allow for root growth. If you have ever bought a sprout from the store, it probably came in a net pot. These are readily available online and are quite cheap to buy.

Tubing

Tubing may be necessary depending upon the pumps that you have chosen out. You should always double-check the tubing that you will need depending upon the system that you have picked out as well. There is not much to this particular step except to avoid clear tubing, as it can harbor algae inside of it, leading to clogs down the road, and that can be a significant problem.

Fertilizer and Nutrient Solution

Perhaps one of the most critical parts of this whole system is the nutrient solution. The solution is what sets this particular system apart from most others, and you need to remember that the nutrient solution that you make use of may vary significantly from plant to plant. You can buy liquid concentrated fertilizer, or you can buy the dissolvable fertilizer that you can mix yourself, depending upon your budget and which you prefer.

Monitoring Equipment

Monitoring your setup is a crucial part of making sure that it is running. For the most part, the only real work that you will be doing after getting your system up and running is monitoring and maintaining. You are likely not going to be doing most of the work of gardening—that is what the system itself. However, you do need to make sure that you are monitoring it to ensure that it will work properly and produce what you need.

These three factors are easily monitored through the use of a thermometer, pH testing kits, and an EC meter.

- **The thermometer** is easy—you can get these anywhere. Keep in mind that you will need to be able to measure ambient temperature, the temperature of the area around the plants themselves, and the nutrient solution.
- **The pH testing kit** can happen in many different ways. You can test with litmus strips—you literally would just dip a strip of paper into your solution and

then compare the color to a scale of colors on a box to tell you more or less what the pH was.

- **The EC meter** is another vital tool. To measure whether or not your solution is the right strength, you test with the EC meter. It will tell you the electrical conductivity (EC) of the solution.

Plants

Finally, the last crucial element of any good hydroponic setup is the plants. You need to make sure that you know which plants you want and how you are going to grow them. These are necessarily your defining factors to your system. If you have chosen strawberries, for example, you are going to grow them very differently compared to lettuce. They will have different requirements, and they will need different setups.

Choosing the Plants

You must choose your plant according to the space available for your hydroponics. Use short crops that you can quickly grow at your patio or balcony and do not take lots of space. There are many varieties of cucumbers, beans, and herbs that you can quickly grow at your patio or balcony. Remember that it doesn't matter whether you grow your plant inside your home or outside; they still need sunlight, water, and nutrient supply for proper growth. Many herbs need sunlight exposure of at least 5 hours a day, so choose a place where you can provide that much amount of sunlight for your herb plants.

Tomatoes contain 70% water and therefore need proper watering to grow appropriately. Still, you don't have to worry about watering in hydroponics, and this is the reason why tomatoes give high yield and why that maybe your best choice for hydroponics.

Flowers are another excellent choice for growing hydroponically. Flowers thrive well in hydroponics, and you can also use them for decorative purposes. You can use tropical and semi-tropical flowers for your hydroponics that generally don't grow in your region.

Anyone who enjoys fresh flowers can enjoy growing some gorgeous flowers in his home through hydroponics.

The only point you must consider before growing flowers with hydroponics are that you can grow only a single species of flower in the single hydroponic system. Most flowering plants have different requirements of nutrients, minerals, and pH levels to grow appropriately, and you cannot mix other breeds with it.

Herbs are the best choice to grow with a hydroponic system because they can snowball and need less care. Herbs can be used for daily consumption purposes, and they also have many medicinal properties. You can grow herbs inside a small hydroponic system and put them on your patio or balcony. A minimal unit of hydroponics is enough to grow abundant crops of herbs that should be enough for your daily consumption.

Make a proper plan of how you are going to use your space and what variety should be beneficial to grow. Choose the fruits and vegetables that your family loves to eat. Choose plants that take different time to harvest and grow the seedlings in advance from 3-5 weeks if you are growing them yourself. You can also buy seedlings from your nearest nursery if you want. You can use a mix of plants that have different harvesting times. Tomatoes take 8-10 weeks to produce crops, whereas lettuce only takes 4-5 weeks.

You can grow practically anything in a hydroponic garden, but some plants are much more fruitful than others. Here's a list of recommended plants to begin with:

Vegetables

- Tomatoes (while a fruit) work very well with drip systems

- Lettuce (and most leafy vegetables) can quickly be grown and cared for with an NFT technique.

- Celery is excellent with an ebb-and-flow type system

- Cucumbers work great with a drip irrigation system

- Radishes can be grown in a direct water culture system

Lettuce

There is a great variety of leaf lettuces that grow exceptionally well hydroponically. There is, however, one exception: the iceberg lettuce. It is because it needs colder temperatures to form a tight head. Iceberg lettuce is therefore not well suited to the backyard greenhouse setting. Besides this, iceberg lettuce has a shallow nutritional value compared to other leafy greens.

The following are some favorite lettuce varieties:

Black Seeded Simpson: Many tend to start the season with this delicately flavored and tender leaf lettuce. It is because the Black Seeded Simpson is incredibly well suited to early spring sowing, yet is well adapted to a wide range of temperatures and climates.

Winter density: This lettuce is compact, tightly folded with an excellent texture and flavor. Its leaves are dark green, and it is well suited to all seasons.

Magenta: This summer crisp is shiny, puckered, has a great flavor and reddish leaves. Magenta is best suited to spring and summer sowing.

Muir: This summer crisp is the most heat tolerant lettuce. The leaves are light green, crisp and have an outstanding flavor.

Nevada: This lettuce has bright green leaves and is ideally suited to spring and summer sowing.

Cucumber

There are many different cucumber varieties. Which variety you should choose will largely depend on growing conditions: temperature, humidity and light condition.

The following varieties are resistant to Powdery mildew. This fungus disease affects a wide range of different plants, and tend to be best suited to humid conditions:

'Camaro,' 'Dominica,' and 'Flamingo.' There are also many other varieties, including 'Bologna,' 'Discover,' and 'Optima.' Because of the full range of different available varieties, it is recommended to try a few different realities and see which ones tend to perform best in your hydroponic garden. With cucumbers, it is best to change crops every 3 – 4 months to ensure you get the most significant yield.

Fruits

- **Cantaloupe** and other netted **melons** work great in ebb-and-flow systems. The melons should be supported with nets or something else.
- **Blueberries** can be planted in a hydroponic garden, but remember that you won't see fruit until the end of the 2nd year. However, they don't need to be replanted!
- **Strawberries** require low humidity and can get root rot, so be careful if you decide to grow this delicious fruit! You'll likely want an NFT system for this.
- **Grapes** can also be grown in a hydroponic garden, but they require a lot of care! A bucket system would be great.

Herbs

- **Oregano**, like most herbs, will work well in a drip or ebb-and-flow system

- **Chives** can also be grown very quickly!

- **Basil** is ideal for a drip or NFT system. It grows fast, too!

- **Sage** is excellent for an NFT setup, or you can put it in other systems.

- **Rosemary** develops best in a drip system (with a soilless potting mix).

Chives

There are two types of chives: regular fine leaf chives and garlic chives, also called Chinese leeks. Germination for both types is within 1 – 2 weeks. Fine leaf chives will continue to grow for a year without replacement and take around 10 – 12 weeks from sowing to the first harvest. Garlic chives take around 12 – 13 weeks from sowing to the first harvest. They can, however, be harvested as soon as they reach 6 – 8 inches in height. When harvesting, however, make sure to leave around 3 inches of a plant from the crown of the plant to stimulate re-growth. The flowers of garlic chives are edible and also make a beautiful garnish!

Basil

Basil is a cooking staple, known for its outstanding aromas. Basil leaves are flavorful and best when fresh. Because of this, it is among the most favorite and sought-after herbs.

Italian basil

The most common basil we encounter is the Genovese, the classic sweet Italian basil. Basil seeds germinate after around 5 – 10 days. The plant itself needs around 9 – 10 weeks to reach maturity but can be harvested after three weeks.

For indoor hydroponics, it is recommended to use basil plants that are FUSARIUM-resistant. Two examples of Italian basils that are resistant to FUSARIUM include 'NUFA' and 'Aroma 2.'

Asian basils

Besides the Italian basil, there are also exotic types of basil that are commonly used in Thai and Vietnamese cuisines. Two varieties include 'sweet Thai,' which grows to around 12 – 18 inches in height, and 'cinnamon' basils, which grow around 26 – 30 inches tall. Both variants take around nine weeks to reach full maturity.

Greek basils

Greek basils, also called fine leaf basils, are most commonly used in pesto, stuffing, soup, and vegetable dishes. They have a stronger flavor than Italian basils. Two favorite Greek basils include 'PISTOU,' which grow to around 6 – 8 inches in height, and the 'spicy bush,' which grow 8 – 14 inches tall and take roughly ten weeks to reach full maturity.

Citrus basils

There are also citrus basils that are often added to salads and fish dishes. They are favored for their distinct citrus aroma, take 8 – 9 weeks to reach maturity, and reach 20 – 24 inches in height.

Oregano

Oregano is a must in on every pizza! The crop reaches around 8 – 24 inches in height over an 11 – 13-week period from sowing to full maturity. Germination occurs within 1 – 2 weeks. Harvesting can begin once the plant reaches around 8 inches in height. Stimulate continuous growth, and it should be harvested every three weeks. Like mint, oregano plants will last for around a year between crop changes, provided it is pruned regularly.

Rosemary

Rosemary germination occurs within 2 – 3 weeks but can be irregular at times. The crop reaches maturity within 4 – 6 months. After 11 – 14 weeks, you can start cutting off the tips of the crop. Rosemary will grow for a year before a crop change is needed.

Sage

Sage reaches maturity at 11 – 13 weeks and can grow 16 – 30 inches long. But the crop can be harvested as soon as it reaches 6 inches in height. The seeds germinate within 1 – 3 weeks. Because sage hangs down, it is important to cut the crop regularly. Regular trimming ensures that the plant remains succulent and productive for a year before a crop change is needed.

Trimming, Harvesting and Reducing Dieback

With all herbs, particularly if grown in a plant tower, regular pruning from the very beginning will reduce competition for light between plants. Regular pruning will also reduce dieback as well as keep the plant lush and productive. If dieback occurs, remove the dead plant material as soon as possible to prevent cross-infection.

To harvest hanging herbs, take a handful, bunch them together, and use scissors and cut across them. It is important here to always leave at least 4 inches of growth (from the base of the plant to the cut) for regeneration. As the plant matures, leave at least 4 – 5 inches of growth when pruning. Don't allow the crop to flower unless you intend to use them for scent or in floral arrangements. A plant should be changed once the interior of the bunch becomes dry and woody. Any dead plant material should be removed immediately to prevent infection.

To summarize, basil, chervil, coriander, dill, and fennel should be replaced after around 3 – 4 months. Thyme will need a crop change after around six months. Chives, lavender, oregano, parsley, rosemary and sage will if regularly pruned, last for a year before a crop change is needed.

Nutrient Solutions

When you grow your plants in the ground, nutrients come from the soil itself and from the fertilizer or compost that the gardener adds to the plant beds. Hydroponic gardens deliver nutrients through the liquid solution in the reservoir. Here you'll learn how plants 'uptake' these nutrients, what those nutrients are, and tips for getting the optimum concentration.

Understanding Nutrient Uptake and Nutrient Solution Tips

Plants need nutrients just as much as you or I do. But just like you or I, plants can be overfed or underfed. Understanding the way that your plants get their nutrients will help you to understand their needs so that you can adequately tend to them.

Nutrients come in two forms. *Macronutrients* are the larger building blocks that your plants need. These can be nitrogen, phosphorus, and potassium; they're primarily mixed to create your nutrient solution. There are also *micronutrients* like boron and chlorine, which different species may need in larger or smaller amounts. For your plants to be able to uptake nutrients, they must first be dissolved in water. While you can easily see how this occurs in a hydroponic system, it might seem odd when traditionally-grown plants get nutrients from the soil. However, you need to water your plants, and it is this action that allows the nutrients in the soil to be dissolved enough for the plants to make use of them.

The roots of the plant suck in the nutrients, and then the vascular tissue pulls the nutrients up the stem and pushes it out through the leaves. All plants have tiny pores (or stomata) covering their leaves, which release water vapors. Its release creates a negative pressure inside the leaves of the plant, which helps in pulling water throughout the plant. In turn, it ensures that nutrients are spread out through the plant as they have been dissolved in the water.

Different nutrients are absorbed in different rates. Likewise, different species require different concentrations of these nutrients. For example, tomatoes like a mixture of 190mg/l nitrogen, 40mg/i phosphorus, 310mg/l potassium, 150mg/l calcium, and 45mg/l magnesium. Nitrogen is a fast-absorbing nutrient, while potassium takes between ten to twelve times longer, and phosphorus takes forty-eight to ninety times longer than nitrogen.

The interplay between these absorption rates primarily comes into play when first mixing your nutrient solution. Since most KRATKY crops use a single nutrient solution to go from seed to harvest, the nutrients are mixed at the appropriate ratio and then left alone. When using a pre-formulated nutrient solution, such as the General Hydroponics nutrients suggested above, simply follow the instructions on the packaging. It is the best approach for new gardeners.

Those growers who are looking to mix their nutrient solution from raw ingredients need to be mindful of the quantities involved. Tomatoes prefer a lot of nitrogen. Strawberries, however, only like to have 50mg/l, which is only a fourth of the tomato plant's requirements. So, the strength of the tomato plant solution would be harmful to a strawberry plant. Carefully study the needs of your plants before mixing your nutrient solution.

When making a nutrient solution from raw materials, use multiple containers for each step.

Use one container to mix your macronutrients and a separate container for mixing

the smaller traces of micronutrients. When each of these has been correctly balanced, then put them together with the water for your nutrient solution. Check the pH level and adjust accordingly.

A Look at Plant Nutrients and Fertilizer

There are three groups of nutrients when considering what to feed your plants. There are primary macronutrients, which will be mixed in the largest quantities and which make up the majority of your nutrient solution (aside from the water). Secondary macronutrients are also important to your plants but are needed in much smaller doses than primary macronutrients. Then there are micronutrients which your plants do need, but only in small amounts. A properly formulated nutrient mixture such as that from General Hydroponics will include all thirteen of these macro and micronutrients. It is these thirteen mineral nutrients that are used to make up fertilizer.

The role of fertilizer in traditional gardening is not to feed your plants directly, despite what you may think. Fertilizer is used to protect the microorganisms which live in the soil that your plants are growing in. These microorganisms are an essential part of keeping your plants growing properly, and they, in turn, help to break down nutrients in the soil and the fertilizer so that it is easier for the plants to use them.

A hydroponic system doesn't use soil. In your KRATKY method system, you are using an inert growing medium. It means that it doesn't have essential nutrients. Nor are there microorganisms that need care. The nutrients are the liquid solution, and the roots of the plant can uptake them readily. The nutrient solution replaces the need for fertilizer in a hydroponic system. Fertilizers are mixed in low concentrations so that they protect rather than harm the microorganisms in the soil. Hydroponic nutrient solutions are mixed much stronger since there are no microorganisms to protect. Still, the solution provides all the necessary nutrients that fertilizer would normally deliver. Thus, you don't need to fertilize a hydroponic system.

Returning to the nutrients your plants need, we have left out three nutrients; these aren't found through minerals. Oxygen, hydrogen, and carbon are all necessary building blocks to produce big and healthy plants. Oxygen and carbon are both pulled out from the air itself, and this is why a breathable growing medium or soil is often used in gardening. The KRATKY method allows the roots of its plants to be exposed to the open air inside the system. So this provides oxygen and carbon easily. Hydrogen is simply just water, and it is the largest ingredient in your nutrient solution.

The primary macronutrients are nitrogen, phosphorus, and potassium, or NPK. Nitrogen helps plants to create protein cells properly, and it makes photosynthesis possible. Phosphorus is used to strengthen the cell membranes inside your plants. Potassium is used by plants to grow because it signals compounds and facilitates cellular movement within the plant.

There are also three secondary macronutrients: calcium, magnesium, and sulfur. Sulfur helps molecules inside the plant to bond with each other more easily. That will help new growth to stay strong. Magnesium is used to facilitate photosynthesis further, and calcium is used to strengthen the plant's cell walls. The micronutrients used by plants are boron, chlorine, copper, iron, manganese, molybdenum, and zinc, and these all play their part in helping the macronutrients effectively function inside the plant.

Learn how to make your nutrient solution and what growing media you can use for your system. An effective hydroponic system will need a good nutrient solution. Here are the steps on how to make your solution.

The ideal hydroponic system is one that is built in a greenhouse; however, it is not necessary. The gardener needs to be able to control the temperature. Hydroponic systems offer food to the plants through liquid fertilizers that are provided to the growing media. The growing media does not contain any soil. Most of the commercial fertilizers only have plant nutrients, which are nitrogen, potassium, and phosphorous. Micronutrients and minerals like iron and zinc are not in the fertilizer due to it being present in the soil; therefore, you will need to add those. Here are ways to make a different nutrient solution.

MATERIALS

- Water
- 1 Gallon – Compost
- 1 Pound – Worm Castings
- ½ Cup – Molasses
- 5 Gallon Bucket
- Air Pump – Aquarium
- Disposable Filter
- Measuring Spoons
- Fish Emulsion
- Seaweed Extract
- Blood Meal

TIPS

The important nutrients for plant growth are hydrogen, carbon, oxygen, potassium, phosphorus, nitrogen, calcium, sulfur, iron, boron, magnesium, copper, zinc, chlorine, and molybdenum.

COMPOST OR WORM TEA

- **Step 1:** Put one gallon of compost or one pound of warm castings inside a five-gallon bucket.

- **Step 2:** Fill your bucket with water and stir it very well.

- **Step 3:** Aerate the mix continuously with an air pump.

- **Step 4:** Let your bucket sit in direct sunlight for three days. Stir it daily.

- Pour the liquid through a filter to strain out any solids. The liquid is your tea and will be used for fertilizer.

ANIMAL OR PLANT BYPRODUCT

- **Step 1:** Add one gallon of water into a bucket.

- **Step 2:** Add in 1-½ teaspoons of fish emulsion.

- **Step 3:** Add in 1-½ teaspoons of some seaweed extract.

- **Step 4:** Add in one tablespoon of a blood meal.

- **Step 5:** Stir it very well and use it as a fertilizer. Use the same ratio when making it on a larger scale.

Chapter 7. Lights and Heat

Lighting for all hydroponic systems is one of the main components. It argues that so many light types exist. If conditions are not the same, any group of plants can respond to lighting very differently.

New farmers find it hard to determine which lighting method is the most suitable. It can be hard to understand, as every lighting device has many different features. It is not a question of providing an old light to plants; it must be the correct form of light, and understanding what light will generate is half of the issue.

There are a lot of lighting choices, so here we go through every form to see how they function and what's special.

Measuring the Lighting System of a Hydroponics

It is useful to see how light is measured and what every bulb has to give before going through various types of lighting.

Light is measured in some ways, but others are practically obsolete, but in other things still used. One such term is the foot-candle or the strength of the candle, and this also refers to torches or light bulbs that shine in millions or thousands of candles.

When you grow in hydroponics and find the ideal light, the temperature is one of the first terms to consider as well. The heat production has little to do with this temperature. Still, it is a reference to the natural color created by light. When we see cold light, it gives light at the blue end of the spectrum, when gazing at warm lights; it gives light at the red/orange finish of the spectrum.

Watt strength, nanometers (nm) or lumens may be most commonly measured by light. The watt power is the power units required to control the lighting and is the word most people know. When it comes to lighting, it is also determined by the number of watts available to illuminate every centimeter.

Lumen reflects the brightness of a rising sun. Although it is used, these lumens are not necessarily a measurement of the plants. The light needed by plants goes beyond the visible physical range.

As nanometers measure light, it is the light we can see. Its visible light ranges between 400 and 700 nm. In contrast with the color spectrum, the warm or the red end reads 730 nm, while the other end reads 400 nm in the colored portion of the spectrum (violet). Far from 450 nm to 730 nm, almost all grow lights dropped. These are the most significant nm steps with a mid-spectrum addition of 650 nm.

We are all aware that plants need to photosynthesize and that light at the 450 nm and 650 nm levels is needed for plants for this reason. Plants thus can produce food from the light and water and carbon dioxide they need. Chlorophyll is made of the black pigment.

It helps plants to regulate the flora through a pigment called PHYTOCHROME as they use the 650 nm and 730 nm levels. It is why at various stages in the plant growth, the full spectrum of light is appropriate, and why it is vital to have the best lights to reproduce this.

However, this is where I elaborate on each lighting system, and see how far they help in the efficient growth of plants, to help you make the right choice for your hydroponic system

Fluorescent Light

For years, these lights have been around, and they are very cost-effective. Another major advantage is that they are cool and can be placed very close to plants without fear of being burned. But even the drawback of these bulbs is illustrated by this plus factor. The light they give out is not intense enough for leaves or leaves to reach past plants. The implementation of the bulb system T5 is one of the latest developments, but there is a range of issues for this type of light.

T5 Lighting

It allows you to find over a dozen size variations. It can be important to know the dimensions of your area to measure the growth space and then determine the needs of your lighting.

Such bulbs are usually two lengths in which they are 2 ft. or 4 ft. Wide. Besides, some fittings may be fitted with 1, 2, 4, 6, 8 or 12 illumination tubes. Once you measure your room, it offers good flexibility. The thumb rule is a small area where a two or a 4 ft. Light with 1 or 2 bulbs is available for a few plants. You'll need a 4 ft. Fixture with more bulbs in wider areas and more plants.

T5 Bulbs

The T5 tube is one of the main draws since it protects various color temperatures. While an exact number that satisfies various criteria for farmers is difficult to provide. The choice of a bulb with 6,500 Kelvin is a good starting point for rising plants. The bulbs with 3,000 Kelvin are best suited for flowering.

6 -8 inches above your plants can be put T5 grow lights. If you have plants or if your plants show signs of aversion, pick this up to 12 centimeters.

What I like about this system

•More cost-effective than other lights

•Multiple and robust forms of the emitted light

•Covers greater areas than most lights

What I don't like about this system

•Not the right alternative during phases of vegetative growth

•Not the right for flora phases

HID Lights for Hydroponic Systems

High-Intensity Discharge Light (HIDs) has much larger lamps than other systems. It functions by a gas being ignited in the bulb. It is achieved with electrodes that sit close, and the gas is ignited by a flow through them.

This form of the bulb can be found in two separate varieties, but the third is a hybrid.

Metal Halide: This burning gas produces light on the bluer end of the spectrum of color. It helps the plant growth process the vegetative phase.

High-pressure Sodium: This type of bulb produces light that is positioned on the red/orange end of the spectrum and ideal for plants that have flowered.

All HID bulbs have the problem of needing other components to be running and working. The following are Ballast – this helps to get the bulb going when it is triggered and also prevents electricity running. Both come in two shapes and magnetic ballast that controls power by using spools and a condenser, and the second is the newer optical ballast. They are more efficient and cost-effective in service.

Reflectors: in the purest form, they are a light stainless steel hood sitting above the bulb to allow light fall to the plants.

After a total of 10,000 hours or more, HID loses its (Lumen) capacity by nearly 70 percent. If you run the lights for fourteen hours a day, it will take about two years to bring this forward. But many growers closely monitor and change their lights well before this time is over.

But these are very powerful bulbs, even if it needs to be changed periodically. They provide the plants with very active UV rays by the sun and, therefore, very efficient photosynthesis.

What I like about this system

•Can be dimmed to provide adjustable illumination.

•Digital ballast enables the application of all HID bulbs.

•Supply better than the T5's available display.

What I don't like about this system

•If put too close, it may burn plants.

•Include additional working components – ballast, reflectors.

•The loose output of bulbs over time – regular adjustments are required.

LED Lighting Fixtures

They have been around for a while but are still new in hydroponics for many farmers. These have many advantages over other lighting systems, although still very costly.

Thankfully, their rates tend to decline as they gain more attention. Many manufacturers, however, produce lights that provide less illumination. See that the lights you want are a minimum of 2.0 micromoles per watt of energy when you want to buy.

Such cheaper LED systems are not adequate to support flora plants, so some housework must be carried out in advance. Depending on the plant form, this will change, but I hope that the subsystems will disappear if costs are reduced.

Lastly, many are sold in one unit when it comes to purchasing LED lighting systems.

What I like about this system

•Very strong, they are one of the cheapest sources of light to operate.

•LEDs produce a little more light per watt energy than fluorescents as well as HIDs.

•The LED runs much hotter, and plants are far less likely to be burned.

•LED's are very long-standing, and even before the bulbs themselves, it is the control panel.

•No ballast is required for the LED to work and can be connected to the power socket directly.

•LEDs display a wide range of colors and can be customized to suit the needs and growth stages of your plant.

•The most easy-to-use LEDs are now established.

What I don't like about this system

•Such lighting systems are more expensive than alternatives.

•Some lighting systems emit less light than others.

Some manufacturers create lights that are not able, when they bloom, to support plants.

How to Set Up Your System At Home

Assembling a Generic System

First, begin by deciding on the location. Set up the hydroponic system in an encased structure, for example, a nursery or the storm cellar of your home, or on a spacious yard or deck. The floor ought to be level to guarantee even the inclusion of water and nutrients to the plants in the system. On the off chance that you are putting the system outside, shield the system from the elements, for example, provide a breeze shield and check the water levels all the more regularly because of water loss from dissipation. During cold temperatures, bring the hydroponic system inside. If you are putting the system in an inside room of your home, add growing lights to give supplemental lighting to the plants.

Stage 1 Collect the Hydroponic System

A basic system comprises six cloning cylinders made of 6" PVC pipe, a stand, and a framework made of PVC, a 50-gallon supplement tank, a siphon, and a complex. The tank sits under the table of 6" PVC developing cylinders, and the siphon sits inside the tank to push supplements up to the plants utilizing a complex of smaller PVC funnels and plastic cylinders. Each developing cylinder has a drainpipe that leads back to the tank. The complex sits over the funnels and sends pressurized water to the cylinders. Get the nutrients to the plants in this system, water is pushed through a square of PVC, the complex. Afterward, it gets shot out to little plastic cylinders that run inside every one of the bigger developing cylinders. The nutrient tubes have extremely little openings in them, one gap between each plant site.

Stage 2 Blend the Nutrients and Water

Fill the tank you have with water. Turn on the siphon and let the system run for around 30 minutes to get the entirety of the nutrients altogether blended.

Stage 3 Add Plants to the Growing Tubes

Probably the most straightforward approach to plant a hydroponic nursery is to utilize bought seedlings, particularly on the off chance that you don't have the opportunity to develop the seeds yourself. The key is to pick the most beneficial plants you can discover and afterward evacuate the entirety of the dirt off their roots.

After the roots are perfect, pull the same number of roots as you can through the base of the planting cup and afterward add extended soil rocks to hold the plant set up and standing. The extended soil stones are hard, but on the other hand, they're light with the goal that they don't harm the plant roots.

Stage 4 Bind the Plants to the Framework

Utilize the plant clasps and string to attach the plants to the framework. The string will give them backing to climb straight up, which boosts the space in this limited territory. Bind the string freely to the highest point of the framework, join the clasps and string to the base of each plant and delicately wind the tips of the plants around the string.

Stage 5 Turn on the Pump and Monitor the System Daily

Check the water levels day by day; in certain areas, it might be important to check it two times per day, contingent upon water loss because of over the top warmth and dissipation.

Stage 6 Screen Plant Growths

It is imperative to watch out for plant development and tie or clasp the plant stalks at regular intervals.

Stage 7 Examine the Plants for Pests and Diseases

One unhealthy plant can quickly taint the different ones since they are so near one another. Expel any wiped out plants right away. Since plants developed hydroponically don't need to burn through their effort attempting to discover nourishment, they can invest more energy developing. It encourages them to be more beneficial and more grounded because they can utilize a portion of that vitality to ward off maladies. Since the leaves of the plants never get wet except if it downpours, they're significantly less prone to get leaf organisms, buildup, and form.

Although hydroponic plants are acceptable at warding off illnesses, regardless, they need to battle bugs. Regardless of whether it's hydroponic, bugs and caterpillars can discover a route into the nursery. Take out and discard any bugs you see.

Building Your Own Hydroponic System

Beginning Plants

Keep the tray on a plot for seepage, yet the seedling shut shouldn't dry out something over the top and seedling should come up in a couple of days. Seedlings can remain on the plate until roots develop from the base or sides of the seedling square. When this happens, seedlings are prepared to be transplanted onto the Rockwool capillary mat in the root chamber. At the point when the system is operational, and plants are developing, within the root chamber ought to have rich, hearty smell. Put three or four plants if you are growing them large (and outside), eight if you're developing quick and blooming early (and under lights).

At the point when the roots develop from the base or sides of the Rockwool block, it's prepared to transplant into the growth tube. When the roots have developed into the capillary mat, you can hit them with full quality hydro juice. Light confirmation plastic ought to be utilized to cover the highest point of the root chamber white side up, and this is to stop the green sludge development on the Rockwool. It must be done when the plant is sufficiently tall, take care not to strain or harm the plant.

Numerous seeds require extraordinary conditions to develop. For instance, most nursery vegetables and herb seeds need to stay soggy or wet for quite a while.

Seeds can be sprouted in a hydroponic cultivator, and regularly they develop far and away better than in soil.

Planting Seeds

Most seeds are set beneath the outside of the media. A recommended arrangement is from 1/2 to 1-inch underneath the surface. It keeps the seed wet and will give it some vibe for when the light is and where the dimness is. The root of the plant will develop down towards the dimness and the water, and the plant stem and leaves will go towards the light.

Many seed parcels incorporate guidelines for soil and tell you how deep to cover the seeds. They can be planted at a similar profundity in hydroponics.

A few seeds, similar to beans and corn, will sprout in only a couple of days. Some others, for example, tomato, chime pepper, and herbs, may take up to about fourteen days until they show up. Cultivators with seeds ought to be watered every day, albeit no plants are appearing. On the off chance that you don't perceive any indication of life following two weeks, it is ideal for replanting the seedling.

Once in a while, the seedling root region will be so cold or so dry, the seeds won't sprout.

To sprout exceptionally little seeds like numerous herbs, a unique type of germination might be required. One route is to begin the seeds between two bits of paper or a towel doused with water. The towel is kept saturated every day.

Growing a few sorts of seeds is more muddled than simply absorbing the water? A few seeds should be harmed somehow to develop, and others are particular to react to times of temperature or light. If there is something you might want to develop, you may want to research what the seed prerequisites are to grow.

Things to Consider When Buying Hydroponics Tools and Equipment

Planning and budgeting is a necessity in a hydroponic garden that prepares you for several outcomes and situations. Buying tools and equipment is an aspect that requires planning not just because of the budget, but because there are other factors to be considered.

What Tools

What type of hydroponics system is being built? The type of system most likely determines the tools and equipment is needed even though most tools used for setting up one type of hydroponic system can be used for setting up a different hydroponics system, very few tools are peculiar to one type of system.

Where to Buy

Deciding where to buy equipment is usually brought up regularly. The questions of what stores to buy from, online or in-store are asked constantly. Whether it is online or in-store, what counts is the reputability of the stores or companies the purchase is being made from, which medium of purchase would be more convenient and hassle-free.

Cost

A budget is required to know the amount that can be spent on tools and equipment that can purchase. Many hydroponics sales websites have the prices of materials and tools on them and sometimes offer free shipping. Planning a trip to a hydroponic store to window shop or for a price survey would also help. For small scale, hydroponics, systems, some tools required can easily be found in the household. A scale of preference could be made, deciding what to spend more money on and what to spend less on or what not to bother. Usually, more money is spent on plant lights, especially if the system is going to be indoors.

Warranty

Buying from a reputable company or buying a reputable brand is important because many of these companies have return policies usually 30-90 days with a money-back guarantee sometimes and warranty on the equipment, ranging from 1-5 years

Maintenance

Maintenance is as important as purchasing the tools and equipment. The equipment usually comes with instructions for maintenance. In buying tools and equipment, ensure the purchased equipment can be maintained to ensure continuous usage. How good the tools and equipment work determine how well the system works.

Common Problems in Hydroponic Systems

Hydroponics is a perfect way to develop difficult, enjoyable, and very enriching plants at home. However, there are a variety of hydroponic problems that you may experience, and it's necessary to learn how to prevent or successfully deal with these.

Use of the Wrong Fertilizer

Some of the necessary micro-nutrients are already present in adequate amounts in the soil when growing plants in soil. For this purpose, fertilizer intended for growing plants in the ground need not contain many of the micro trace nutrients that are important for healthy plant growth.

Solution

Make sure you buy nutrients intended for hydroponic use.

You can make your hydroponic fertilizer from scratch, but buying a two-or three-part solution is much simpler. It can be combined to create a nutrient solution that can be adapted to most plants and phases of growth.

Not Keeping Things Clean

Part of the cleaning cycle is to avoid the ability of bacteria, viruses, and pests to develop them in your environment. While some people run systems explicitly designed to promote the growth of beneficial bacteria, I think it is best to prevent pathogenic species by cleaning the system and surrounding area regularly for most home hydroponics setups.

Solution

Keep clean and well organized the area around your hydroponics system.

Drain the machine every 2-3 weeks, flush the rising media and roots with water and purify the tank, pumps, and tubing.

Not Monitoring the Health of Your Plants

If you don't regularly monitor your plants, you will miss the early signs of problems. If this is inadequate growth or signs of deficiency or illness, the sooner you know that there is a problem, the more opportunity you have to fix it and not kill your plants.

Solution

Regularly track the growth and condition of your plants.

Take the time to know what the problem is when you see a problem and try to fix it.

When you find a disease or pests, treat them early, and you can be able to avoid unnecessary plant damage.

Not testing and changing the pH Level

One of the most important aspects of hydroponic growth is the pH level of your nutrient solution. The soil itself serves as a pH buffer when growing plants in soil, which avoids sudden shifts in the pH level. That means pH issues are quicker to develop and can be managed more easily.

With hydroponics, that is not the case. The pH will change dramatically over hours or days due to several factors including temperature, rate of nutrient absorption by your plants, presence of disease, and excess evaporation.

Solution

When growing with hydroponics, you need to control the pH of your nutrient solution.

You may need to check and update the pH regularly in a new program, or when recent improvements have been made.

The simplest way to test pH is by using a pH test kit or a pH test meter. I generally recommend having an electrical pH test meter of decent quality, since it makes pH testing fast and simple.

Blocked or Defective Pumps and Spray Nozzles

Hydroponics systems depend on daily or very frequent water and nutrient delivery to your plants. If you have a malfunction or blockage of the pump or nozzle, this can very easily lead to problems.

A damaged or blocked water pump may cause the plants to be cut off from their water source in most systems. Wick and DWC systems are not going to have that problem.

Air pumps can fail, too. It doesn't take too long for the plants to allow the dissolved oxygen levels in the water to drop to a point where the roots start rotting, which can allow them to die.

Solution

A regular test of the system

Consider purchasing built-in warning water or air pump, which will sound if a blockage occurs.

Try developing the device, so that it won't lead to rapid plant death if there is a blockage or failure.

For example, for NFT technique systems, a reasonable alternative is to keep the water outlet at the end of the channel slightly elevated, which will result in a small pool of water that will remain in the event of a pump failure.

Choosing the Wrong Growing Medium

Most rising media can be reused; others are only suitable for once use. Others are absorbent, and retain water around the roots of the plant. Some are minimally absorbent and permit swift drainage. Others are costly, and others are cheap. Many growing media can be modified to function in different hydroponic systems, and their preferences would be different growers.

Solution

Take some time to consider what the rising media needs to do.

Read around to find out what others have been most effective.

Consider your budget, and if you want several through cycles to reuse the media.

Not Flushing and Refilling the System Often Enough

The problems of hydroponic growing plants are worth it altogether. If you decide to run your machine too long before flushing it and adjusting the nutrient solution, there will be a major increase in the risk of having problems, or even losing your crops.

Solution

While hydroponics is substantially less labor-intensive than soil-based gardening, more frequent monitoring and adjustment is needed. Flushing the machine and transferring the solution to the nutrient is a bit of a hassle, but it is worth it. More abundant produce, faster-growing plants, and greens for my kitchen all year-round are the benefits I'm getting. My system is worth some essential routine maintenance. As I gain experience, I become more active and reliable in my ability to adjust the nutrient solution, flush the system, and clean my reservoir.

Plant Diseases

In general, hydroponic plants are less susceptible to disease than soil-growing plants. Without soil, there is less space for bacteria and fungi to establish themselves.

Solution

To prevent disease in your hydroponic plants, seek to eliminate conditions under which the pathogens thrive. It means avoiding extremely high temperatures and humidity levels, and ensuring that your plants receive enough direct sunlight or artificial light of good quality.

Track the pH of your nutrient solution and its concentration. Make sure your nutrient solution contains all the necessary macronutrients and micronutrients your plants need for growth.

Quite much check the plants for any symptoms of the disease. Try to find the cause if you encounter a problem, and handle it as soon as possible.

Building an Inconvenient Hydroponics System

Many factors can make a hydroponics system more inconvenient. It can become difficult to place a device in a small space without enough room to work around it or to position it somewhere where your equipment isn't close to hand. A device that has no convenient source of water can cause you to regret down the road. A poorly designed DIY system that's prone to leakage or failure can just frustrate you.

Solution

Start small if it's a DIY system or a pre-constructed system; the first few rising cycles should be treated as learning. You will move on and plan something different time if you make poor decisions at the start.

Prepare your hydroponics system–You need to have your equipment and water supply near at hand. To the device, so you can prepare a nutrient solution or clean your equipment.

Tips and tricks

Tips and Tricks to Growing Healthy Herbs, Vegetables and Fruits

To get the optimum results out of the hydroponic system, you must know the right way of growing hydroponic plants so that they will yield more crops. Many individuals quickly get disappointed with hydroponic gardening, amateur growth, and as they are beginners. However, the reason for this disappointment can be one of these:

Lack of ability- for hydroponics system, you need experience, or you don't have sufficient equipment or supplies.

Unorganized- you know everything regards to hydroponic gardening, but you want to put forth the maximum effort into it.

May be lack of knowledge- means you don't have enough experience concerning hydroponics gardening.

Let's put some light on the varied hydroponic tips and tricks in below points by which you can become an expert and fulfill your dreams:

1. Choosing the right type of crop

In the technique of the hydroponic system, almost every plant can grow. Still, as a beginner, you can start with small plants by which you gain knowledge and experience.

The first step is to choose those plants which need less maintenance and nutrients. As a beginner, you can take herbs and vegetables. Therefore, growing small plants can improve your experience as well as learn new things which are best for the future when you produce other plants.

2. Make a proper plan

When you make up your mind to plant a specific type of crop in your hydroponic garden, the following step comes is planning. Means knowing varied kind of nutrients which are essential for plant, various equipment, and photoperiod. So that you have a full overview of how it can offer better results.

Make a list of every small to the massive thing before planting a crop.

3. Why and when to test and adjust the PH level in hydroponic plants

Every plant which you plant in your hydroponic garden only absorbs nutrient solution in the PH if the answer is in between the range of plant which you have planted. However, if the PH is not up to the mark, then it won't matter how much your nutrient solution is, the plants will suffer from malnutrition and will die after some time.

For beginners, it is recommended that they will check the PH of the plants daily for the best results.

4. Have proper and sufficient lighting

When you search the market, you will get countless types of grow lights according to your budget.

The types of lighting are:

High-intensity discharge (HID) is suitable for extensive hydroponic gardens that have good airflow and proper air condition.

Compact fluorescent lights (CFL) offer good results in small rooms.

Light-emitting lights (LED) are also best for small hydroponic gardening, but they are more expensive than CFLs.

Whatever, you opt to make sure that it will discharge light between 401 and 701 nanometers.

5. having control on temperature

It is one of the essential tips of hydroponic gardening. If the temperature of the plant exceeds 85 degrees, the overall growth of the plants will stop quickly. If the gardener is using HID lights, then it becomes challenging to control the temperature.

For maintaining the accurate temperature, the gardener has to install centrifugal fans. Still, in some cases, the fans alone cannot solve the problem.

For this, plan hydroponic gardening when the outside temperature is 55 degrees or less. Therefore, it is possible to pull fresh air in the garden. On the other hand, you can install air conditioning.

6. The right type of equipment

First and foremost, one thing which you need to consider before setting up a system of the hydroponic garden is to have proper and unique tools. Like in the dark area, hydroponic gardening system, an oscillating fan, TDS meter, maybe an air conditioner, and a digital timer.

7. Select an appropriate nutrient

You have to gain knowledge with regards to varied nutrients, which are crucial for plant growth when you start gardening. Side by side, an individual must know about the number of nutrients required by diverse plants or which plant you have grown.

8. The health of the roots

The health of the root is essential for the overall growth of the plant. Time to time check the origins of the crop so that plants will not suffer from any damage. While offering nutrients to the plants minimizes the amount of light so that algae and fungus will not damage the roots of the crops.

9. Offering water to the plants

This tip is one of the crucial ones because overwatering the plants will damage the crops. In reality, the water intake of the plants depends upon the type of plants means whether it is small or large.

Crops that grow on dry season need more water than crops that grow in a humid climate. On the other hand, some plants hold moisture for a long time as compared to other plants. So, while planting a crop, see whether it needs more water or less so that you can set up the water draining system.

10. Maintain the humidity level

Various plants have a different level of humidity on which they can survive on their development. So, keep in mind that plants will grow faster and yield higher crops when they are given the proper level of humidity.

11. Airflow and ventilation should be proper

For the healthy growth of crops, airflow is a very vital part, which also aids in maintaining the overall temperature of the plants. Fans and air conditioners should be installed in appropriate areas so that plants will be healthy.

12. Understand PH first

The understanding of PH level in plants is must get successful in hydroponic gardening. Interestingly, some meters can take the PH readings, but on your side, you also have to understand this. The main reason for checking the PH level of plants is that water doesn't have a proper range of PH by which plants can die or suffer from malnutrition.

13. Make liberal use of your pruning shears

Any time of the day when you see something on the plant, just prune it away, it can rot the full plant. The cleaner you keep your plant higher the yield.

14. Think about the taste of the fruits or vegetables

In this regard, which fruit or vegetable tastes excellent when it is purchased from the market or plucked from the hydroponic garden?

The main motive of doing this is an end number of crops that don't have a different taste. Either they are purchased from the market or plucked from the garden. Before deciding to choose the crop to plant, give priority to those fruits or vegetables that taste better when they are freshly harvested from the garden.

15. Take care of space and type of hydroponic system

Well, it is fascinating to grow crops such as corn, melons, and squash. But the point is they need ample space. Make sure that you choose the right system and appropriate hydroponic kits. There are countless factors, like ventilation and water, which are crucial elements that make the hydroponic system successful.

16. Always plant fastest-growing, most natural cultivation, and most crucially which offer high yield

In this field, you have learned as much as you can, depending upon your capability. It is the only way by which you can decide which the right crop for your hydroponic system to use. Find out the seeds which are cheap and yield high so that your profit margin is also high.

17. Explore vitamins B

Many of the beginners in hydroponic gardening ignore the impact of stress on the plants. If you see that your plants are not suffering from any of the diseases, then also, they can face stress issues. So, if you think that your plants are facing stress issues, offer them vitamin B supplements that are safe, and with that growth will surge significantly.

These above tips are a basic one, especially for beginners who say that hydroponic gardening is complicated.

Hydroponic Growth vs. Soil

With an immensely growing population all over the world, food resources are consuming even faster, leading this world to food shortages and resource shortages. Under such horrible conditions, a technology like Hydroponics needs to be put into practice for good plant growth without having to wait longer as we do for the soil growing process. Apart from these, there are a lot of reasons why hydroponic cultivation is more convincing and possibly better than soil cultivation. From saving time, money, effort and whatnot, to be more productive in growth, growing hydroponics is a better way than growing soil. Hydroponic growing has proved to be better in many ways; some of them are described below:

GETTING STARTED AROUND MUD:

Hydroponic growing seems increasingly convincing if you consider it the better and modified form of cultivation soon, not only because it is environmentally friendly and environmentally friendly, but it will take all the traditional ways of farming that bring too much mud into the environment and spread but is much more economical than that of conventional harvesting and growing methods.

And yet the best part is that many people have switched to growing hydroponics, have had better results and more seemed to take advantage of their lower costs, new and affordable hydroponics systems. They took full advantage of stable long-term profits.

In addition to being super eco-friendly, hydroponic growing is also economically preferred over soil cultivation, causing a muddy mess in the environment.

HARVESTING ON A LIMITED SPACE GROWING:

When you need a way out to boost the harvest without expanding your harvest space, growing hydroponics may be just what you were looking at all. Its technique allows you to rise as much as you want, even in a limited area, unlike soil growing techniques.

SAVE MONEY AND PREVENT FROM MONEY LOSS:

By switching from soil technology to hydroponics, you ensure a money-saving tragedy and save yourself from potential money loss in a way that conventional farmers working in business must purchase herbicides and establish an herbicides budget that has been exceptional over the years has risen. Farmers have to grow outdoors, and the poor farmers have no option to increase the herbicide ratio, leading to enough money loss. On the other hand, by growing in a sustainable hydroponic environment, you only need to supply selected raw materials to individual plants, in fact with weeds that have too little or no chance of setting up a shop where they don't belong, so that is a lot of savings in the long run and therefore risk reduction.

GET DIRTY WHEN BEAUTY IS THE KEY:

No doubt, growing with hydroponics is much cleaner than growing with soil; let's think there would be no dirt stain and no labor for cleaning purposes. Is it not so easy to continue with such work? Exactly, so if cleanliness is your priority, then make hydroponics your priority, above soil growth that will lead enough to know insects, no parasites and nothing. At the same time, the soil is that medium that can grow these pesky and irritating varieties.

WITH YOUR DESIRED PH VALUE:

Because you have to work with the hydroponic technique, you have your setup for PH under control, unlike in soil cultivation. Plants grow well at a lower pH, such as 5.2 to 5.9 and above that range. Plants can reduce growth. That way, growing hydroponics can be more efficient for plants.

CONSERVATION OF WATER IN A GREENHOUSE:

A study at the University of Arizona found that soil-grown crops tend to consume ten times water as hydroponically grown crops, which is basically with roots allowing growing in nutrient-rich water and fertile soil. By switching your crops from soil to hydroponics, you can drastically increase your efficiency, not only that, but that can also reverse water to harvest your plants again. You can also store gallons of water by growing with hydroponics.

PREVENTING DISEASE AND PROVIDING BETTER PEST CONTROL:

What if you have no idea where all those insects, parasites are, maybe under the piles of dirt, right? So you need to get rid of such insects, which require switching to the cultivation of hydroponics from soil since there is no dirt involved in hydroponics. Not only this but if you can prevent pests from entering your crops as well, causing root rot, powdery mildew, grubs and other ailments, which have the potential to transition from one year's growth, making it for small farmers who recover from pests. Hydroponics technology also allows you to prevent crop contamination from being transferred from crops to crops.

PRODUCTIVITY AND BIGGER HARVESTS:

Hydroponics not only make your harvesting cycle faster, more protective and less time consuming, but also offer a lot of harvest and subsequent cultivation within the limited area and limited resources. Hydroponic gardening is indoors, where these environmental factors such as temperature, humidity and available light are all controlled, allowing hydroponic growers to create ideal environments that are sustainable for specific plants, helping to produce more abundant harvests.

CHEMICALLY FREE PLANTATION:

Plants that grow without soil are less suspected by the threat of diseases and other parasites, and by eliminating the soil, you also reduce as many diseases as possible.

Most pests are more susceptible to the weaker plants. With hydroponics, there are very few more vulnerable plants that somehow amazingly translate to fewer pests. It seems crazy, but ridiculously right and means that far fewer sprays are needed.

YIELD OF CROPS:

Crops are potentially growing fast. According to a NASA study, studies seem to show that the immense potential of hydroponic growing techniques is growing more quickly compared to that of soil cultivation.

FAST GROWING INSTALLATIONS:

Hydroponics crops have been extensively proven to grow 50-70% faster than those grown in soil.

WIDE DIFFERENT CULTIVATION GROWTH

Humans have managed to grow a wider variety of plants, not just herbal plants, such as strawberries and pumpkins.

There is no work in the science of hydroponics, and much of the current focus is on the implementation of existing hydroponics. As a form of cultivation, Hydroponics is mainly funded by those involved in private sector economic growth, depending on the goods they market. Another disturbing consideration is that the Hydroponic Society of America, after the conclusion of its last trials in 1997, was not involved. The company was founded in 1979 and organized annual meetings and publications between 1981 and 1997. When considering current hydroponics, the impact of economic and technological progress on society cannot be overlooked. For example, the possibility of air and land transport of goods ensures that food products can be produced far from their point of consumption.

The emergence of plastics has had an enormous impact on hydroponic materials, as growing vessels, liquid tanks, drip irrigation tubes, greenhouse glazing materials and cladding materials - essential components for all hydroponics and greenhouses operations - come from a wide variety of plastics that vary in physical or chemical properties.

Computers and computer systems have revolutionized the decision-making and control processes for values of every aspect of a hydroponic/greenhouse business. Even if you can deduce that the development of hydroponic crops is gradually becoming a science, a lot of art is still needed to make this plant growing technique both a challenge and an adventure.

Hydroponics VS Aeroponics

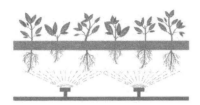

In hydroponic cultivation, as mentioned several times, plants are grown in the absence of land and with the use of water. In general, it is possible to say that with this technique, plants grow thanks to the action of water enriched with nutrients. In a first period, the plants are started inside inert substrates, such as coconut fiber, perlite, expanded clay, or other materials useful for the realization of substrates, to then pass into hydroponic systems, which provide, in addition to correct water supply, thanks to the presence of ad hoc lamps, the temperature, humidity and the right ventilation of the environment.

AEROPONICS is an alternative form of growing plants, vegetables, and fruits that do not require the use of land or water.

With this cultivation technique, plants live and grow brilliantly and hearty thanks to the nebulization of a nutrient solution, based on water and substances useful for growth, which is delivered to the roots with a special spray.

This technique should not be confused with hydroponics, where the most crucial element is not air, as in this case, but water.

Once the AEROPONICS system is set up, the plants are suspended with the roots in the air inside a grow room (or cultivation chamber) where they will remain until the moment of collection.

The basis of growth and plant health is undoubtedly the constant control of temperature, humidity, and lighting.

Pros and Cons of Hydroponics

We have already said several times that the advantages of using a hydroponic system certainly concern reduced maintenance, the possibility of cultivating at any time of the year, and the opportunity to control the climate of the cultivation environment.

More generally, the great advantage of hydroponics is in complete control over nutrients and, therefore, on the growth of plants. Furthermore, hydroponically grown plants perform better than plants grown in the soil. Many systems of this type recycle water and reduce waste.

These soil-free cultivation systems use only 10% of the amount of water needed for conventional crops. They are fairly easy to build and assemble. Hydroponic gardens do not require the use of herbicides or pesticides, precisely because weeds do not grow there, they need little space. They do not depend on the growing seasons, because they use lamplight, which can be installed anywhere.

However, hydroponic gardens have some cons; for example, if the temperature is too high or too low, even for a single day, the plants could die or otherwise suffer severe damage. Also, the purchase of hydroponic systems and accessories may require a significant expense, especially if you are not an expert.

Pros and Cons of AEROPONICS

Among the advantages of AEROPONICS, there is, in the absolute first place, the efficiency and cleanliness of the cultivation environment.

With this technique, excellent and thriving crops are obtained in a short period. Another significant advantage is the slight risk of contracting bacterial diseases and infections. On the other hand, a disadvantage, especially if you are a beginner, lies in the rather high cost, because it requires the purchase of a series of equipment. Also, it is necessary to have a dedicated indoor room, where you can install the AEROPONICS system.

Hydroponics and AEROPONICS**: similarities and differences**

The hydroponic and AEROPONICS systems have many points in common: AEROPONICS is, in reality, a particular type of hydroponic culture, which also uses the benefits of air. To simplify and summarize, we can say that AEROPONICS is an evolution of hydroponics, to get the most out of the potential of plants in terms of yield and speed.

The main difference between the two techniques is that hydroponic systems come in many forms: plants can be suspended in water full time, or a continuous or intermittent flow can feed them. In a hydroponic system, plants grow with water and without soil, with the help of inert substrates. The two systems have in common the supply of nutrients that are delivered directly from the source and supplied to the roots.

The plants in AEROPONICS, however, are never placed in the water but sprayed at a distance thanks to a dispenser that hydrates and nourishes the roots several times an hour, thanks to an automated system that guarantees regularity and punctuality. One reason these two cultivation methods have so much in common is that AEROPONICS is, in reality, a type of hydroponics. The main difference is that hydroponic systems can be of various types: there are different types, and for this, you can choose the one that best suits your needs.

A disadvantage common to both hydroponic and AEROPONICS cultivation systems is that relying on automated systems that require, therefore, electricity, they could require the use of expensive generators to be used in case of power outages. However, once set up and started, hydroponic and AEROPONICS systems allow you to save significantly compared to traditional cultivation techniques.

According to current phenomena, it is possible that forms of hydroponic and AEROPONICS agriculture will increase in popularity over time and become commonplace in all of our homes. What is certain is that due to climate change and the unregulated action of man, the quantity of soil available for cultivation will tend to decrease, and its quality will continue to deteriorate. Therefore more and more people will try to produce healthy food in their homes (many have already started to grow salads, tomatoes, and strawberries). Hydroponic and AEROPONICS gardens and orchards can provide the right answer to these growing needs.

What to Expect When Planting Your First Hydroponic Plants

All plants and crops go through a three-phase lifecycle. The first phase of this cycle is known as 'germination.' It is when a formerly dormant seed starts to sprout a seedling or shoot. Seeds need a warm (approximately 80°F or 28°C), water-rich environment to germinate, but don't need light to do so.

The second phase is known as the 'vegetative phase.' Plants spend most of their life in this phase. During this time, the plant dedicates all of its energy to grow its roots, stem, and leaves (and it needs a lot of nitrogen to do this).

The third phase is called the 'flowering/fruit phase.' During this phase, the plant expends all of its energy on producing flowers or fruit (and because of this, it needs a lot more potassium and phosphorus).

Although all plants go through these three phases, each type of plant experiences these phases differently.

The Life Cycle of Basil

A basil seed will complete the first phase of its life, germination, within about a week or two after planting.

The second phase of a basil plant's life cycle involves its stem growing about 12 inches in height. You can already start to harvest your basil plant while it is working hard on reaching this height by carefully cutting off leaves along the top of the plant (just be sure to leave the smaller, younger leaves at its base alone). After growing 12 inches in height, your basil plant will slowly start producing less and fewer leaves (so be sure not to prune off leaves from your plant more than once a week during this time).

In the third phase of its life cycle, a basil plant will stop producing leaves altogether and start producing purple or white flowers. You shouldn't harvest the plant's leaves during this time (mainly because they lose much of their aromatic flavor during this part of the plant's life cycle).

The Life Cycle of Lettuce

Lettuce seeds germinate when they're watered and kept at a temperature of about 75°F (24°C). These seeds will start sprouting two to 12 days after first being watered, completing the first stage of their life cycle. Some studies suggest that germinating lettuce seeds in alcohol may increase their yield in life, so consider sparing some vodka for your crops.

The lettuce will then start forming the 'rosette' which will ultimately be its head. Keeping lettuce at cooler temperatures (about 50°F/15°C) during this stage has been proven to increase the fleshiness and bulkiness of the lettuce's leaves, which means that it might be a good idea to invest in a cooling system if you're looking to produce top quality lettuce.

Lettuce should be ready to harvest about 45 days after emerging from its seed's casing.

Ninety days after germinating, lettuce is likely to start flowering. Lettuce flowers resemble dandelions and are not entirely unpleasant to look at all. These flowers will probably stick around for about a month. One of the cool things about lettuce flowers is that they will open when your lighting system switches on (or they're placed in the sun), and close when they're no longer in the light. The seeds inside of these lettuce flowers will be ripe (and ready for re-planting) about two weeks after the flowers first bloom.

The Life Cycle of Strawberries

Strawberries like to take their time, both in producing fruit and in germinating. Strawberries seeds should be placed in full sunlight (or under a lighting system) in a warm area when germinating. These seeds should start sprouting two or three weeks after first being watered. Just remember to keep them in a moist environment as strawberry seeds are particularly vulnerable to dehydration.

Strawberry plants typically produce fruit for the first time about a year after being planted. You'll notice your strawberry plant beginning to produce white flowers, and about a month after this, your strawberry plant should begin producing fruit.

A strawberry plant will be at its most productive when it's about three years old, after which its production will slowly start declining. Strawberry plants typically only live for about six years.

The Life Cycle of Spinach

Spinach seeds sprout about a week after first being exposed to moisture. However, they could take longer to germinate if your growing area is overly moist or warm. These seeds germinate best between 60°F and 65°F (15°C to 18°C) and, unlike strawberry seeds, do not need light to germinate.

The first thing you'll notice after germination is your spinach is starting to grow two long, thin leaves. Don't panic; you haven't accidentally planted the wrong crop! The typical spinach leaves which we love to eat will appear a few days. Be sure to keep your spinach plant at a temperature between 50°F and 70°F (10°C and 20°C), or else your plants may become stunted and stop growing.

Spinach grows incredibly fast, and it should be ready to harvest about a month and a half after germinating. If some of the leaves look large enough to harvest before then, go ahead and pick them. Your plant won't mind in the least.

The Life Cycle of Tomatoes

Tomato seeds need the right climate and moisture to grow. You should germinate tomato seeds at temperatures between 70°F and 80°F (20°C and 27°C). Your tomato seeds should start sprouting about a week after first being introduced to the right conditions.

After germinating, the tomato plant will sprout two cotyledon leaves. However, these should be replaced after a few days of growth by the plant's mature leaves.

Tomato plants produce beautiful yellow blossoms, which eventually produce fruit. If these blossoms fall off of your tomato plant before producing fruit, it may be a sign that your plant is lacking nutrients, or is perhaps being exposed to temperatures that are either too low or too high.

Tomatoes, like spinach, grow incredibly fast and should produce their first fruit about a month and a half after germinating (or two months for new fleshy varieties).

The Life Cycle of Cucumbers

Cucumbers do not like the cold, and their seeds will simply refuse to germinate at temperatures below 50°F (10°C). To germinate cucumber seeds, you should keep them in a moist environment at temperatures above 75°F (24°C).

After germinating, the cucumber reaches its vegetative stage. At this point, you should start encouraging your plants to vine around a plant cage to avoid any mold or fungus, which might result from the cucumber's shoots being exposed to the same levels of moisture as its roots. You should avoid touching your cucumber plant while it's wet, as these plants become incredibly sensitive (and bruise easily) when exposed to moisture.

Cucumber plants produce trumpet-shaped yellow flowers. Of these flowers, those not located along the stem (as these are male), will produce fruit. Cucumber plants need extra care and protection during their fruit phase. They will absorb a lot more water (and may require additional nitrogen supplementation).

Cucumber plants should produce their first fruit about a month and a half to two months after germinating.

The Life Cycle of Blueberries

Blueberry seeds are notoriously shy and take quite a bit of time to germinate. However, you should see your blueberry seeds sprouting about a month after first introducing them to moisture. These seeds should be germinated at a temperature of about 60°F (15°C).

Once germinated, after its vegetative phase, blueberry bushes will start producing small clusters of about a dozen little white flowers. These blossoms eventually become blueberries.

Blueberry bushes should produce their first blueberries about a year after being planted, but take up to five years to reach their maximum level of production. Blueberry bushes live about 30 years, which means that you'll have more than 20 years of top production from one blueberry plant.

The Life Cycle of Beans

Bean seeds that are exposed to moisture and temperatures of about 75°F (24°C) germinate in about eight days.

The bean plant's vegetative phase will see it turn into either a dense bush or a long, climbing vine (depending on the variety which you have planted). These plants will then produce small white blossoms.

The bean plant should produce its first beans about 45 days after it germinated. Bean plants are fantastic producers, because the more beans you harvest, the more beans your plants will grow.

Once your bean plants stop producing the white blossoms mentioned above, it's time to rip them out and start all over again. Bean plants only produce for one season, so there's no point in keeping them around after they've stopped producing new bean pods.

The Life Cycle of Peas

You should soak peas for about two days to rehydrate them before introducing them into your hydroponic system. After that, they should take approximately two weeks to germinate fully. The resulting shoots should start producing their first tiny leaves less than a week after germination. You should start wrapping your pea plant's vines around a plant cage when its stem reaches a height of about three inches (eight centimeters).

Once your pea plant has matured, it should start producing purple blossoms. It should occur about three or four months after germination. Snap and sugar peas should produce harvestable pea pods just over a week after flowering. In contrast, garden peas take up to 21 days after flowering to reach this stage.

Just like bean plants, pea plants are only good for one season, and thus you should remove them from your hydroponic system when they're no longer producing new pea pods.

Conclusion: Hydroponic Gardening Secret

Thank you for making it to the end. Hydroponic growing is becoming increasingly popular as this is a great way to grow plants in a limited area. Plants are grown in a medium containing a specially formulated nutrient solution. The fact that plants grow in a nutrient solution rather than in the soil ensures that they get everything they need to be perfectly healthy. Growing hydroponic plants is not necessarily an easy task, and it takes a lot of support to do it properly. One of the first things you should do is find out where to get the correct information and supplies. You should also know how to choose hydroponics stores where you can get everything you need.

The best hydroponic grow shops will give you advice on the correct type of growth medium to use. Different plants have to be cared for differently. You should also use the correct type of nutrients that best suits your plants. Certain fertilizers are better suited for growing many leaves, while others are better suited for preserving flowers and fruit. Careful selection of hydroponic bearings ensures that you buy fertilizers that are as pure as possible so that your plants receive the proper nutrition at the proper intensity.

Your hydroponic garden is also infested with many pests, especially fungal mosquitoes. Keep this in mind when choosing hydroponic storage because you need the best solution to this problem. It is best to deal with a business that offers biosecure solutions to your problem. It is especially important if you are growing fruits and vegetables in your hydroponic garden, as it is best not to contain any toxic materials.

You also need special lighting to give your plants the proper lighting they need. There are different types of lighting systems from which you can choose. The company you choose should be able to customize the systems you need at a very reasonable price.

There are many great hydroponic stores to deal with. Still, you should choose one that gives you the best selection of pest control equipment, fertilizers, and solutions. With everyone's help, you can create a very lush garden for private or commercial use.

Like all organisms, plants need food to grow and develop. So it is understandable that a well-fed plant grows faster and stronger than a malnourished plant. Choosing the right plant food helps your plants develop. Still, it also makes them healthier and subsequently more resistant to disease.

Essentially, all fertilizers contain the same three main ingredients; these are nitrogen, phosphorous, and potassium. However, several specialty plant foods contain a large number of additional ingredients such as iron, calcium, and magnesia, the balance of which affects particular suitability for certain plants.

Generally, the amount of nitrogen is the most important part of a formula and often an important part of grass fodder. Phosphorous is also important, but it does the job of improving rooting and speeding up the flowering process. As such, food with a larger phosphorous component is more suitable for flowers and vegetables. Potassium is also important for root development, but it also helps increase the size and amount of fruit or flowers.

Food is delivered to plants much more directly within hydroponic systems. Therefore, it is important to discover a suitable solution for your plants. Some may argue that mixing hydroponic solutions with organic food is good practice, but it is wrong for most growers.

Ultimately, as a hydroponic gardener, it is possible to obtain a variety of different specialty foods, which have often been developed for use with a particular form of growth medium. For example, hydroponic nutrients are best used with media such as perlite, rock wool, or clay pebbles. Mineral-based formulas are best suited for direct absorption by plants using another example. Coconut nutrients are the answer if your hydroponic system uses the coconut medium.

Another consideration for those trying to find food for hydroponic plants is the water they use in the system. The soft and hard water supply, as well as the universal supply for more neutral conditions, is available on the market today. Finally, these foods adjust the pH of the system to a level suitable for plant growth.

Starting your own hydroponic system will allow you to eat healthy food, with minimum effort and expenses. This book was made to teach how to make such a system in the simplest way, giving you all the required information to grow a successful hydroponic garden. Remember that you can grow your vegetables using hydroponic, and plant in your garden other types of fruits using the companion gardening technique and, if you don't have much space, using containers, and mix this way different types of techniques for a beautiful and thriving garden!

Printed in Great Britain
by Amazon

59043935R00142